LUNCH HOUR
and other plays

These four plays are comedies in which fantasy and reality each have their own kind of truth.

The author writes: 'the tragic hero struggles with reality and is overcome; the comic slides on the world like a banana skin. In both cases the fall represents a kind of victory.'

In the plays – two of which were written for the theatre and two for television – John Mortimer shows himself not only master of both media, but also one of the foremost 'entertainers' of today.

The photograph on the front of the cover shows the BBC Television production of David and Broccoli *with Esmond Knight as Broccoli (left) and Diarmid Cammell as David. It is reproduced by courtesy of the BBC. The portrait of John Mortimer is reproduced by courtesy of the Camera Press Ltd*

D1189167

LUNCH HOUR
AND OTHER PLAYS

BY

John Mortimer

LONDON
METHUEN & CO LTD
36 ESSEX STREET WC2

These plays are fully protected by copyright. All inquiries concerning performing rights, professional or amateur, readings or any other use of this material should be directed to Peters and Ramsay Ltd, 14 Goodwins Court, Covent Garden, London, WC2

First published 1960
© *1960 by John Mortimer (Productions) Ltd*
Printed in Great Britain
by W. & J. Mackay & Co Ltd
Chatham, Kent
Cat. No. 2/6294/1 (paperback)
2/6436/1 (hardbound)

Contents

Two Plays for the Theatre

Two Plays for Television

Contents

Part One for the Theatre

Two Plays for the Theatre

The tragic hero struggles with reality and is overcome: the comic slides on the real world like a banana skin. In both cases the fall represents a kind of victory.

These plays are intended to be comedies. The first two are on the subject of love. It is difficult to be in love and consistently tell the truth: particularly hard if the only time you have is the lunch hour. Usually lies told for the sake of love are harmless, and only become dangerous as they lurch accidentally near to reality. Telling the truth is often a great concealment; we are given away by what we pretend to be. This, at any rate, was the idea I had in writing *Lunch Hour. Collect Your Hand Baggage* represents another pitfall in contemporary love, that of conferring yourself as a favour – a gesture apt to recoil in ways both humiliating and absurd. It was written with another, larger play in mind: a play in which the youthful characters would play a bigger and more destructive part and the central figure more fully represent, than Crispin, the errors of experience. However, in writing it I became fond of Crispin. In the beer age, when he flourished, we stood in draughty pubs instead of warm and comfortable coffee bars. The doors swung open and out of the rainy blackout came tottering elderly women whose Slavic cheek-bones were once alleged to have been modelled by Epstein. Dylan Thomas had only just left. And there, of course, was Crispin, his overcoat, in which he slept, hanging open: someone else's cigarette in his mouth, desperate, lonely, ready to discuss the latest number of *Penguin New Writing* with the next available deserter from the W.R.N.S. Or perhaps he was happy with the long-haired girl he had met in Charlotte Street during an air raid, or at the

National Gallery Concert, or walking under the blue sky and silver barrage balloons round the Ministry of Information. How would such a character survive from the sentimental, hopeful 1940s into the cold, clear, despondent world of today? Perhaps he could become a kind of hero, a symbol of some idiotic and indestructible adolescence. Sufficient of a hero, at any rate, to trip over the truth of what has happened last night, and fall flat on his face.

J.M.

Lunch Hour

LUNCH HOUR was first broadcast in the BBC Third Programme on 25 June 1960, with Wendy Craig as the GIRL and Stephen Murray as the MAN. It was produced by Martyn C. Webster.

The play was first performed on the stage at the Salisbury Playhouse on 20 June 1960, with Nancie Herrod as the GIRL and Patrick Kavanagh as the MAN. It was produced by Robert Cartland.

Cast

THE GIRL
THE MAN
THE MANAGERESS

As the curtain rises a clock is striking one on the mantelpiece of a small hotel bedroom in the neighbourhood of King's Cross Station. It is winter.

The door is back stage, centre. Almost the only article of furniture is a large, brass-ended double bed with a white cotton cover. Otherwise the room is dingy yellow, the peeling wallpaper decorated with a recurrent pattern of castles. There is an unlit, shilling-in-the-slot gas fire, a naked electric bulb hanging from the ceiling, and, on the mantelpiece beside the chiming clock, a Bible and an ABC of trains. There is a noise of trains from outside, and a thin curtain is drawn across the window. The GIRL *enters and looks cautiously round the room. She is perhaps twenty-two, dressed as an office girl with artistic interests.*

The MAN *follows her in and switches on the pale bulb from the door. He is nearly forty, with thinning hair, indecisive good looks, a business suit and a stiff collar. He and the girl are both wearing overcoats. They have no luggage.*

As she looks round the room, the GIRL *begins to laugh gently.*

MAN. Why're you laughing?

GIRL. I don't know.

MAN. You're happy?

GIRL. I laugh when I'm hungry too.

MAN (*disappointed*). If you'd rather eat . . .

GIRL. Not at all. (*She throws her arms round him.*) You look so big in that overcoat . . . like a house.

MAN. I'll take it off.

GIRL. Not yet. What's this place?

MAN. Just a hotel. . . .

GIRL. A hotel?

MAN. By the station. It's convenient. . . .

GIRL. What for?

MAN. The north of England.

GIRL (*dreamily*). You say the most ridiculous things. . . .

They kiss.

And no one knows we're here?

MAN. I'm having a long business lunch with the textile buyers in the Tudor Room . . .

GIRL. And I'm alone with an open continental sandwich in a dark corner of the coffee bar with the rubber plants brushing my cheek and the out-of-work actors staring like hungry jackals at the big Italian waitresses in the small black trousers . . .

MAN. And I'm saying: "Well, gentlemen, have a large plate of smoked salmon on the Commissioners of Inland Revenue."

GIRL. But if they looked for us in those places . . .

MAN. They wouldn't find us.

GIRL. No, we're nowhere. . . .

MAN. We're here.

GIRL. We've disappeared . . . We don't exist.

MAN. For an hour . . . or longer!

GIRL. No.

MAN. Business lunches stretch out endlessly.

GIRL. You can't spend much time on an open continental sandwich.

Pause.

MAN. You look so small in that overcoat.

GIRL. What do I look like?

MAN. A child in the park on a snowy morning. A woman who's disguised herself to run away to sea. . . .

GIRL. Go on talking. . . .

MAN. The inexperienced wife of an Arctic explorer. . . .

GIRL. Go on!

MAN. I've run out.

GIRL. What of?

MAN. Words.

Pause.

GIRL. As a matter of fact they're quite good, those sand-wiches, and they have other things, too, hamburgers, hot franks in soft floury rolls, great tubes of mustard. Such up-to-date and convenient food!

MAN. You'd rather be in the coffee bar?

GIRL. This is much more . . .

MAN. What?

GIRL. Exciting.

MAN. You mean that?

GIRL. Because I love you.

MAN. And me!

GIRL. How long?

MAN. Since the day you walked into my office . . .

GIRL. With the new design for bedspreads.

MAN. Spanish ivy!

GIRL. You remember!

MAN. And said: "Is this the way to the duplicating depart-ment?"

GIRL. And you said, "No."

MAN. But I'd show you. . . .

GIRL. And you rose up with the light from the window behind you so you appeared all silver, like a shining statue . . .

MAN. And I took you to Mr. Jevons . . .

GIRL. Down the long dark corridors, past the rude and elderly stares of the typing pool . . .

MAN. In the lift.

GIRL. You didn't say a word!

MAN. We certainly established sympathy. . . .

GIRL. You being so quiet in the lift was what I appreciated. Not saying any vulgar remark such as "Where have you been all my life?" or "Is there another one at home like you?" Not even looking. . . .

MAN. I was genuinely impressed!

GIRL. Yes.

MAN. And you seemed so lost and uncertain. Like I sometimes feel in that great organization.

GIRL. What words . . . from the head of the textile buying department!

MAN. Only the policy director.

GIRL (*holding on to him*). Oh, love! How it attacks you!

MAN (*thinking of his work*). I'm only the Number Two in that slow-moving department. Blast Harris!

> *He kisses her almost absent-mindedly, and she breaks away from him.*

GIRL. You don't think I'm the sort of girl who comes to a place like this?

MAN (*giving her all his attention again*). No!

GIRL. Then why'm I here?

MAN. My fault.

GIRL (*shakes her head thoughtfully*). That must be the sort of girl I am.

> *Train noises.*

What's that?

MAN. The station.

GIRL. I'm the sort to come here. (*A thought strikes her.*) And what about you? Is this how all your lunch hours are passed, with some girl or other, and you have to creep out of the office at four o'clock every day for an enormous great high tea?

MAN. I've never been here before.

GIRL. Honest?

MAN. Yes.

GIRL. I'm sorry.

MAN. I love you.

GIRL. Say it again. . . .

MAN. I love you.

GIRL. Yes.

MAN. For six months. . . .

GIRL. All through the summer.

MAN. With nowhere to go.

GIRL. In spite of the office and your . . . home life.

MAN. It kept us alive.

GIRL. When we had only a few moments; standing by the tea trolley in the corridor.

MAN. Holding hands in the lift. . . .

GIRL. You waiting for me in the Embankment Gardens, always first out of the office, being on the executive planning side. . . .

MAN. Always the same bench!

GIRL. With the flowers standing straight as soldiers and the one-stringed fiddle playing in front of the tube and the tramps asleep under their sheets of newspaper. We had ten minutes a day, now we've got . . .

The clock chimes a quarter.

MAN. Three-quarters of an hour.

GIRL (*moving away from him, and round the room*). In this room.

MAN. You don't like it?

GIRL. It's not all that sordid really.

MAN. We could make ourselves more at home . . . take off our coats.

GIRL. It's cold.

MAN. I'll light the gas. (*Goes to the gas fire.*) It needs a shilling . . . (*He can't find one.*) Damn!

GIRL. I'll look. (*She burrows in her handbag.*) Only sixpences. Would it take two sixpences? (*She puts them in the fire . . . no gas.*)

MAN. Now you've lost your money.

GIRL. It really doesn't matter.

MAN. Let me give it back to you.

GIRL. It couldn't matter less.

MAN. By the end of the week you'll be short of a coffee.

GIRL. No, really.

MAN. Here. (*Counting money to give her.*) Sixpence . . . sevenpence . . . ninepence. . . .

> *There is a quick knock at the door and the* MANAGERESS *enters. Meanwhile the* GIRL *is almost shouting.*

GIRL. I don't want your money!

MANAGERESS. Did you want something? (*The* MANAGERESS *is a large woman, motherly and concerned.*)

MAN. Ah, yes, a shilling for the gas.

MANAGERESS (*to the* GIRL). You're cold. A journey does make you cold. Much snow up there?

GIRL. Up where?

MANAGERESS. The north of England.

MAN (*hastily*). Just a powdering of snow, didn't you say, darling?

GIRL (*bewildered*). I haven't any idea. . . .

MAN. The train was going too fast to take a good look.

MANAGERESS. An express?

MAN. That's it.

MANAGERESS. They *can* be fast. Was it the *Scotsman*?

GIRL. Was what?

MANAGERESS. The *Flying Scotsman*. My little boy collects engine numbers. Many a time he's seen the *Scotsman*, waiting at the end of the platform. Puffing and blowing. Would you like a cup of tea?

MAN. Not at all.

MANAGERESS (*to the* GIRL). Wouldn't you?

GIRL. Well . . .

MANAGERESS. Isn't that husbands for you? Never appreciate the plain and simple fact that what we wives need after a long cold train journey is a home-made cup of tea. Much snow, did you say?

MAN. She had lunch on the train. . . .

MANAGERESS. That doesn't take the place, dear, does it?

GIRL. What of?

MANAGERESS. A cup of tea. (*She is going.*)

GIRL. Just a. . . .

MAN. Very quick cup.

The MANAGERESS *goes.*

GIRL (*lost and puzzled as she turns to him for an explanation*). Where've I come from?

MAN. Scarborough.

GIRL. Why?

MAN. I told her that was where you lived.

GIRL. Why should I live in Scarborough?

MAN. Because you're married to me.

GIRL (*accusingly*). Then why don't you live in Scarborough too? What's the matter with you? Can't you stand the climate? You delicate or something?

MAN. I've got digs in London.

GIRL. Thank you very much!

MAN (*patiently*). It's the housing shortage. I've simply got to be near the office. So you're living with your mother in the north!

GIRL. Charming!

MAN. Naturally, it's a long journey and you don't get up to London very often. . . .

Knock.

Come in.

The MANAGERESS *comes back with a cup of tea.*

MANAGERESS. Drink that down and you'll feel the benefit. You must be worn out!

MAN. She's not very tired. . . .

MANAGERESS. But they *are* a strain. On a long journey. . . .

L.H.—B

GIRL. What are?

MANAGERESS. Running up and down the corridors. Poking their noses into the first class. Playing with the chickens in the guard's van and locking themselves in the toilets.

GIRL. It's like a sort of dream. (*She sits on the bed, lost and confused.*)

MANAGERESS. Never seen London before? This is their first glimpse of the smoke?

GIRL. What's she saying?

MANAGERESS. Their first tube and double-decker? If I know anything, that'll mean the Chamber of Horrors for you this afternoon, unless their Aunty . . .

GIRL. Is she out of her mind?

MANAGERESS. You know what mine does on a long journey?

GIRL. How can I possibly tell?

MAN. Well, I think you've finished your tea.

GIRL. It's hot.

MAN. You don't want it?

GIRL. Might as well. . . .

MANAGERESS. On a long journey mine always takes out his box of crayons, and chalks the marks of an infectious disease on his face before the journey commences. . . .

GIRL (*puzzled*). What for?

MANAGERESS. To ensure privacy in the compartment. . . .

GIRL (*interested*). Does it work?

MANAGERESS. Nine times out of ten. And if not . . .

GIRL. Yes?

MANAGERESS. He can make it pretty sticky for those that do venture in. But why I mentioned that rogues' gallery was this. When his cousins come on a visit from the north, it's always down the stairs at the Tussauds they make their first port of call. . . .

MAN. Ours doesn't like that sort of thing. Finished your tea, darling?

MANAGERESS. They don't like Tussauds?

MAN. Gentle, nervous children, weak on history . . . You'll want to wash up the cup? (*He takes the cup from the* GIRL *and gives it to the* MANAGERESS.)

GIRL. Who are we talking about now?

MAN. Our children.

GIRL (*breathless*). How many?

MANAGERESS (*accusingly*). Three.

GIRL. Three?

MANAGERESS. Two boys and then your husband got his girl!

GIRL. Congratulations!

MAN. Time's passing.

MANAGERESS (*leaving with cup and saucer*). I've got things to do. They'll be excited, though, seeing Aunty after all this time. . . . (*She goes.*)

GIRL. Who's Aunty?

> *She rises accusingly to her feet. The* MAN *tries to kiss her, but she turns her face away. She repeats insistently:*

WHO'S AUNTY?

MAN. My married sister. She lives near the Heath.

GIRL. Is that a good thing?

MAN. It's a godsend, as I told the Manageress. She can look after the children. . . .

GIRL. They're with her now. . . .

MAN. She's quite capable . . . a trained nurse, that's what she used to be.

GIRL. Well, I should think they must be totally confused in their small minds.

MAN. Confused?

GIRL. Bewildered.

MAN. But why? . . .

GIRL. For God's sake. What's it all about? Those quiet gentle little children with no sense of history are woken out of their warm beds at what must have been a cruelly early hour in Scarborough, and dragged all the way to London only to be

dumped with some ex-matron of an aunt while we scurry off
to a small private hotel in King's Cross! And another thing
about those children . . . where are they going to spend
the night?

MAN (*guiltily*). I thought . . .

GIRL (*challengingly*). Well? (*Pause, then the* GIRL, *incredulous,
says.*) You can't mean . . .

MAN. You'll all want to get back.

GIRL. To SCARBOROUGH?

MAN. Well, it is home. Only temporary, of course.

GIRL (*rushing to the mantelpiece, she seizes the* ABC *and turns up
the pages with bitter determination*). Scarborough. Saxmund-
ham. Scalby . . . Scarborough! Pop. forty-three thousand
nine hundred and eighty-five. Early closing Wed. London
two hundred and three miles! Four hundred and six miles a
day you would laughingly see me travel with three young
children who can't be all that grown up and responsible,
bearing in mind that fact, which you very well know, that I
am exactly twenty-three. . . .

MAN (*miserably*). The boys were twins.

GIRL. You know what! I DON'T THINK YOU'RE FIT TO HAVE
CHILDREN! I can't think why you went on breeding, for the
selfish reason of wanting a girl after the twins, and, when
I've given birth to them and all that, you can only think of
sending them on pointless and exhausting train journeys
practically the whole length of the British Isles. . . .

MAN. Listen!

GIRL. They'll be dropping asleep by the time we get home,
and suppose we can't find a taxi. . . .

MAN. Please, let me explain. . . .

GIRL. Four lives you've got in your hands.

MAN. I was desperate!

GIRL. THEN WHY COULDN'T YOU COME UP AT THE WEEK-END?

The clock chimes the half hour.

MAN. There's so little time. . . .

GIRL. Such inconsiderate behaviour!

MAN. Do we have to talk?

GIRL. I certainly think you owe me an explanation.

MAN. I'm in love with you.

GIRL. You have odd ways of showing it. If that's the way you treat all your wives!

MAN. You're not my wife!

GIRL. That's one consolation.

MAN. We love each other!

GIRL. What about it?

MAN. Let's be thankful! Let's celebrate the revolution! The victory against the dull and unaffectionate rulers of our lives! Look at this room! Look what we've achieved!

GIRL. What?

MAN. A beachhead in a dark grey enemy country! A small clearing in the jungle behind our own impermanent and wobbling stockade. A place on our own! Does it matter what I had to say to win it for us?

GIRL. Sometimes it matters.

MAN. What?

GIRL. What you have to say.

MAN. It doesn't matter.

GIRL. Anyway, I'm curious to know.

MAN. What?

GIRL. How you got us here.

MAN. Later on. . . .

GIRL. No, now! I want to know exactly who I am. I puzzle myself at the moment.

MAN. Well, I was walking along the street and I happened to catch sight of this hotel. It seemed small and . . .

GIRL. Unostentatious?

MAN. So I was faced with a problem. How could a man and a . . .

GIRL. Woman?

MAN. Exactly! Without any kind of luggage . . .

GIRL. We've got no luggage!

MAN. Come here for an hour, in the middle of the day . . .

GIRL. Your only time for adventure.

MAN. That was the problem. I solved it!

GIRL. You did?

MAN. After a little thought. I said we wanted somewhere to talk. . . .

GIRL. To what?

MAN. To talk.

GIRL. It's incredible. . . .

MAN. The Manageress understood.

GIRL. She hadn't got to face the endless journey back with three uncontrollable children . . . Anyway, we could have done that in the lounge.

MAN. What?

GIRL. Talked.

MAN. No privacy.

GIRL. Or at your married sister's . . . the one who lives up by the Heath.

MAN (*hesitatingly*). Well, no . . . we went into that. It wasn't at all a practicable idea.

GIRL. Why not?

MAN. Well, there's no point in digging up that old buried hatchet.

GIRL. What?

MAN. You see, you've never got on with my married sister.

GIRL. Never?

MAN. She stayed away from the wedding.

GIRL. Oh did she?

MAN. Since then there's been a bit of an east wind between you.

GIRL. I'm not surprised!

MAN. Just one of those little failures of understanding that happen in all families . . . It wasn't at all your fault. You certainly did your best. I told the manageress that, but, well, there it is.

GIRL. What a lot you told that Manageress!

MAN. To get the room.

GIRL. I suppose so.

MAN. All for that.

GIRL. Yes-s. (*She looks at him, long and searchingly.*)

MAN. Because I honestly loved you. (*He kisses her.*)

GIRL (*absently*). Yes. . . . (*She breaks away from him suddenly.*) What's she got against me, anyway?

MAN. Who?

GIRL. Aunty.

MAN. Nothing.

GIRL. What kept her away from the wedding then?

MAN. Well, you know how people are, old-fashioned ideas.

GIRL. You mean you *told* her?

MAN. What?

GIRL. About this afternoon?

MAN. Where have you got me now? (*He looks at her in confusion.*)

GIRL. Where've you got yourself? Do you ever stop to ask yourself that? I mean, whose side are you on anyway? Hers or mine?

MAN. Yours, of course. . . .

GIRL. Well it doesn't look so very much like it! Keeping up such friendly relations with a woman who wouldn't even condescend to turn up at the reception my father can ill afford, leaving our children to the tender mercy of this starched and creaking old matron with her grey moustache and celluloid cuffs who treats me (*She is crying.*) like a nasty mess in the out-patients! I should have thought you might show a little more honesty and integrity and act more like the bright shining husband in glittering armour that you let me think you were when you tricked me . . .

MAN. I tricked you?

GIRL. You let me believe I was the only thing that mattered in your life.

MAN. You are!

GIRL. Now it seems any old aunt gets more consideration . . .

MAN. IT'S NOT TRUE!

GIRL (*a pause. She is sobbing in his arms*). I'm sorry.

MAN. I'm sorry too.

GIRL. You are?

MAN. I'm sorry we had to have all these . . . complications.

GIRL. I didn't mean you tricked me.

MAN. I know you didn't.

GIRL. I just thought you might write to her, that's all.

MAN. Write?

GIRL. Nothing abusive, of course, nothing to bring us down to her level.

MAN. Whose?

GIRL. Just, "In view of your attitude, it would no doubt be more convenient if you let at least twenty years elapse before paying your first call." You never wrote her a line like that?

MAN. Hardly. Because . . .

GIRL. You never came out in the open in support of me?

She moves away from him.

MAN. Because . . .

GIRL. And who is she anyway? (*Her anger returns.*) Trained nurse! What's that? Florence Nightingale? Madam Curie? What's her great achievement? Rolling up some royalty in a blanket bath? Being present at the removal of a so-called appendix from a so-called film star in a nameless Nursing Home in Hammersmith? I know those trained nurses! Heartless! Knit and gossip all night and drink cocoa in the face of death! Just let her try and hold down my job which isn't just automatic and calls for some creative imagination!

We do two hundred versions of the Spanish Ivy pattern now . . . and not one of them a repeat!

MAN. I know.

GIRL. Well, you should appreciate that.

MAN. Don't worry about her.

GIRL. Why not?

MAN. She's not real. . . .

GIRL. She's real to me! Snobs! That's one thing we don't tolerate in our family, thank God. That's one type of person that just seems to me so low that I couldn't get any lower if I got down on my stomach and wriggled under that door. My father's been an ordinary printer for the best part of thirty years, but there's only one type of person that he wouldn't give house room to in any circumstances, and that's a SNOB. Also, he can't put up with the Welsh. But he's never been the sort to go poking and prying into someone's past history and drawing aside his skirts and refusing to attend the ceremony of marriage and turning young children against their mother when her back is turned.

MAN. Look at me!

GIRL. Yes?

MAN. We're alone.

GIRL. Well?

MAN (*urgently*). Remember. Nothing else exists. Everyone else in the world has faded away. All our friends and families and relations. We're alone here together. Fixed and solitary in this moment of time. No one can come near us.

After a quick knock, the MANAGERESS *enters.*

MANAGERESS. I've found a shilling for you! (*She goes to the gas fire and puts it in.*) Now. Who's got a match?

The MAN *hands her a box in silence. She lights the fire.*

There now! That makes it more cosy and homelike, doesn't it?

Pause.

I always say, after a nice coal fire I like a nice gas fire.

Pause.

Of course, you'll hardly be needing all that shilling's worth, now will you?

Pause.

You'll be Good Samaritans to the next occupants.

Pause.

A nice fire is nice to talk by, and you'll want to go on with your discussion.

MAN. Yes.

MANAGERESS. If you give me that change then.

MAN. We had two sixpences.

GIRL (*after searching in her handbag*). We put them down the slot.

MAN. I've only got ninepence, after the taxi.

MANAGERESS (*stonily*). Well, you asked me to get the shilling. I distinctly heard you.

MAN. Yes, we did.

MANAGERESS. Naturally I assumed you had change to give me for it.

MAN. I've got a pound.

MANAGERESS. That's hardly very convenient. How can I change a pound at short notice?

MAN. I don't know.

MANAGERESS. I had to *send out* for the shilling!

GIRL. We've given you a shilling already.

MANAGERESS. What?

GIRL. My two sixpences, straight down the slot, with no result at all!

MANAGERESS. Really . . .

GIRL. You can't expect to get any more out of me.

MANAGERESS. Me? I'm not making a penny! That goes straight to the North Thames Gas Board.

GIRL. With the price of the room, add on two shillings for gas. . . .

MANAGERESS. I've never had any complaints before.

GIRL. How much was the room?

MAN. Well . . .

GIRL. Tell me, how much?

MAN. Two guineas.

GIRL. For an hour!

MANAGERESS. It's no concern of mine if you have to leave after an hour.

GIRL. Two guineas an hour! Forty-eight guineas a day for a broken-down old bed and peeling wallpaper and a gas fire that's daylight robbery and the use of a chiming clock and the ABC of trains! We're in the wrong business! I knew it didn't pay to be creative. . . .

MANAGERESS. I've had twenty-five years in the King's Cross area as a manageress of this private hotel and I've never heard words like that spoken to me before.

GIRL. Well, it's about time. And what about that little boy of yours?

MANAGERESS. What about him?

GIRL. Playing round the station. Going round all the telephones and pressing the button Bs, I should think most likely.

MANAGERESS. I've a very good mind . . .

GIRL. I'm perfectly sure there's some law . . .

The clock is chiming three quarters of an hour.

MANAGERESS. I put myself out to get you a little warmth . . .

GIRL. Some people work for their living!

MANAGERESS. Because you've had a long day!

MAN (*in despair, forcing the pound note on the* MANAGERESS). Take this! Don't come back with the change. . . .

MANAGERESS (*going*). Peeling wallpaper! I tell you, I've had government officials sleep in this very room. Indian gentlemen. And very nicely spoken. Only I was sorry for the fix you and your husband was in. I agreed to take you for the hour. He wanted to talk to you, you see. On a serious matter! WELL HE MIGHT!

She leaves.

MAN (*pause*). I thought we'd never get rid of her.

GIRL (*pause*). Well, she's gone now.

MAN (*pause*). We've only got fifteen minutes left. . . .

GIRL. Now it's coming.

MAN. Won't you take your coat off?

GIRL. I dread it.

MAN. Why? . . .

GIRL. I'm sorry. I know it's silly and stupid and weak of me, perhaps. But ever since I was a child, quite a young girl, you understand, this has been something I have dreaded and I knew it was coming the moment I stepped into this room. I know that was why you brought me here. But whatever good reason you may very well have had, I don't want it to happen.

MAN. But we discussed . . .

GIRL. It's just a horrible feeling I get in the pit of my stomach, just a sick old feeling of waiting and despair. I've felt it coming on and perhaps that was why I was a bit sharp with that old girl, although heaven knows when you have to count every penny, and sometimes travel on the tube with nothing but a cheerful wink at that thin Tottenham Court Road collector, it makes you sick to see money demanded on that exorbitant scale! However, if anyone says to me, "Could I have a word with you?" it's always and quite certainly the one word I don't want to hear.

MAN. What do you mean?

GIRL. The head designer may say: "I'd like a word with you

in the office," or my father says: "We'd like to talk to you if you can arrange to be home early next Wednesday," or they say: "This underground ticket looks a bit exhausted, could we talk to you about it?" and I stand and grin and sweat into the palms of my hands, and whatever it is they have to say I don't want them to say it, so please forgive me if all I can think of at this moment is I DON'T WANT YOU TO TALK TO ME!

MAN. I'm not going to talk!

GIRL. What do you mean?

MAN. You've got nothing to worry about.

GIRL. Why did she say that, then?

MAN. Say what?

GIRL. That you wanted me . . . for a serious talk?

MAN. Please listen.

GIRL. No!

MAN. We've got so little time, and if this goes wrong . . .

GIRL. What?

MAN. What've we got left?

GIRL. It seems I've always got the children. . . .

MAN. Don't you see, you're the one oasis in the desert of my days and nights. The one person that's saved me from suddenly growing old and tired among the bright red hang-it-yourself wallpaper and the Scandinavian lampshades and business lunches. So if we have a few minutes . . . don't waste them.

GIRL. No.

Pause while they come together.

I did love you. When you stood up so silver against the light. . . .

MAN. Please. . . .

They are in each other's arms.

GIRL. And when I got out of the lift and a draught of air from the print room blew up my skirt I saw you turn away your eyes and spare me the look of curiosity . . . and I thought . . . . here's someone quite exceptional in this building riddled with intrigue and romance. . . .

MAN (*kissing her*). Oh, God. . . .

Pause.

GIRL. What were you going to say?

MAN. When?

GIRL. I mean, it must have been something of great importance.

MAN. It was nothing.

GIRL. To bring a person all that way on the train to hear it . . .

MAN. Nothing.

She leaves him and stands back from him, looking at him carefully, as if seeing him for the first time.

GIRL. I mean, you're not the sort of man that wants a woman to travel all that way just to discuss the weather, are you? It must have been something serious and terrible you had to disclose.

MAN. I never thought . . .

GIRL. And all through that long journey! What about it? Hour after hour, watching the frozen lines, trying to keep the children quiet. All the time the thought going round in my head . . . he's got something to tell you. What's it going to be? What's so bad it can't be stuck in an envelope or said out over the telephone? Are you the sort of man that would keep a woman in suspense like that?

MAN. Of course not.

GIRL. But it must be days ago you asked me to come up. How do you think I've been feeling since then. DO YOU THINK I'VE HAD MUCH SLEEP? DO YOU CARE?

MAN. Don't you understand?

GIRL. Not yet. You haven't told me yet. Let's face it now. Let's get it out of the way at last!

MAN. There's nothing to say.

GIRL. Or are you the sort of man that would bring his wife all this way to tell her something of great importance which might affect their whole lives, and then shut up as tight as an oyster the moment he was in her presence?

MAN. No!

GIRL. Coming to look at you clearly with the light in front of you, I think that's the sort of man you might be.

MAN. I'm not. Listen!

GIRL. Because it can only be one thing, can't it? For me to have come all this way to hear it, it can only be one logical thing.

MAN (*interested in spite of himself*). What?

GIRL. That we're finished. That it's over. You don't care about us any more. Oh, it was very convenient for you, having me tucked away at the end of a long cold railway line! It gave you plenty of scope to cultivate your friendships in the office. To take girls down in the lift and lure them into strange hotels during the lunch hour. You were able to take full advantage of the two hundred and three miles you so carefully put between us. So now you'll write a letter starting, "No doubt this will come as a terrible shock to you . . ." which you want me to hand in to give you your so-called freedom. Isn't that what it all comes to, if you had the courage to put it into words?

MAN. I never thought of that!

GIRL. Yes, you did. When you started to talk to the Manageress! When you told her the story. The story had to end, didn't it? Can you think of a different ending?

MAN (*after thinking*). There must be one, somewhere.

The clock begins to chime.

GIRL. Two o'clock. It's over. (*She looks at him with tenderness and pity.*) You should never have explained our presence.

She is going through the door.

MAN. Wait. Wait a minute. I'll tell you why I asked you to come down. I'll tell you what I wanted to say.

But she has gone.
The MAN *looks round the empty room. He stoops and turns off the gas fire.*

We never took off our overcoats!

Curtain

Collect Your Hand Baggage

CRISPIN (*halting them by the* SWEEPER, *looking round the silent place, and saying, to no one in particular*). Thank you all for a loyal and lovely welcome!

SWEEPER (*resigned*). You lot again? (*Pause.*) Cold night. Very airy.

CRISPIN. We're young. We don't feel it.

SWEEPER. All right for you in that overcoat. (*He feels it.*) Nice bit of Harris that. Heavy.

CRISPIN. I'm not selling it. Not yet.

The SWEEPER *goes off, following his broom.* CRISPIN *and his friends move over to the coffee bar and are arranging themselves on stools when the uniformed* OFFICIAL *comes up to them.*

OFFICIAL. Where are you for, sir?

CRISPIN (*amazed*). You new here?

OFFICIAL. Why?

CRISPIN. Where are we not for! Now where shan't we go to tonight? Paris, Uruguay, the draughty and pock-marked back of the moon?

JANE (*tired*). Let's not go anywhere. Let's just stay here.

CRISPIN. Do we *look* the sort of people who'd entrust themselves to aeroplanes! Can you imagine *me* hurtling through space?

OFFICIAL. Well, sir . . .

CRISPIN (*patiently*). Haven't they told you yet. Well! (*To the girls.*) He's young!

SUSAN. Don't disillusion him. . . .

CRISPIN. I'll let you into a secret . . . You collect all these people's suitcases and they pile into those noisy great machines, and the Captains roar them to the far-off ends of the runways and then . . . they stop. Dead! And the Captain comes over the inter-com (*He imitates the Captain's voice.*) "This is your Captain Rogerson speaking. Now none of us really wants to go flying about the sky, do we? I mean,

we're not that mad. So what do you say we kip down here
for the night and in the morning we'll all send postcards
addressed from foreign parts ? . . ."

OFFICIAL. What ?

CRISPIN. They haven't told you that ? (*Comfortingly.*) Perhaps
you're just not high enough up in the organization. . . .

OFFICIAL. Have you checked your luggage, sir ?

CRISPIN (*embracing both girls*). This . . . is all the luggage
I possess. . . .

SUSAN (*wriggling away from him*). Do you mind ?

JANE. I'm Bill's luggage. (*She holds* BILL'S *hand.*)

MICHAEL (*sarcastically*). How sweet!

> CRISPIN *looks dashed for a moment, then he claps the*
> OFFICIAL *on the shoulder and says, reassuringly*:

CRISPIN. Cheer up! Just go on collecting passengers and pre-
tending they're for *some destination*!

> *The* OFFICIAL *shrugs his shoulders and leaves, looking at*
> CRISPIN *with some pity.*

MICHAEL (*to the* WAITRESS). Evening, Liz, darling.

LIZ. You again. The gilded youth!

BILL. So it is.

LIZ. Beats me why you lot come all this way out to the airport
every evening. . . .

MICHAEL. To see you, Liz!

LIZ (*ignoring him*). Coffee ?

MICHAEL. Coffee, everyone! Coffee, Crispin ?

CRISPIN. What . . . (*He is sitting on a stool, looking suddenly
tired.*)

MICHAEL. Crispin!

CRISPIN (*anxiously, to* LIZ). There's a plane for Paris, I suppose, at midnight ?

LIZ. The night flight.

CRISPIN. That's what I thought (*He sounds depressed.*)

JANE. *Look!* What he's given me.

SUSAN. It's a wedding ring!

BILL (*apologetically*) We've used it before. . . .

JANE. But it's a presentation. (*Doubtfully, to* BILL.) It *is* a presentation, isn't it?

BILL (*holding her hand*). Yes. (*Then apologetically, to the others.*) She gets these mad ideas. . . .

JANE. It's to announce our engagement.

SUSAN. It's quite moving . . . in an obvious sort of way.

MICHAEL. It's not *serious*?

JANE. Why not?

CRISPIN. Well, you're doing it wrong . . . A wedding ring ought to be fumbled for, in church, from what I remember.

MICHAEL. A sad ceremony!

JANE. Why shouldn't we get married? People do it . . . all over the place.

BILL. I know it *sounds* obvious, but it might turn out rather unusual!

JANE. After the finals, I mean, we must do something . . . We need a home. . . . (*To* MICHAEL.) We can't go on borrowing your room in the afternoons for all eternity. That studio couch. With the springs falling out of it. . . .

BILL. While you and Susan go and sit in the Baker Street Classic. . . .

Their words have been rising in speed and excitement, until CRISPIN *says suddenly in a gloomy voice:*

CRISPIN. Marriage!

BILL. You're against it?

CRISPIN. It's like a journey, by air! To go to the airport is the best way of spending the evening! But to take off is . . . merely vulgar!

JANE. You never married?

CRISPIN. I won't say never.

JANE. Where is she?

SUSAN. Your dark secret. . . .

MICHAEL. You never told us.

SUSAN. Tell, Crispin . . . tell, tell.

A LOUDSPEAKER. WE NOW ANNOUNCE THE DEPARTURE OF OUR FLIGHT NUMBER FIVE O FOUR TO ATHENS AND TEHERAN. . . .

SUSAN. The East . . . (*She puts a paper table napkin like a yashmak round the bottom part of her face, her eyes peering large and Eastern above it.*) You met her in the Cas-Bah!

MICHAEL. On the way home from that drunken orgy with the British Ambassador. . . .

SUSAN. She was being auctioned in aid of the Turkish Red Cross. . . .

MICHAEL. And you put in a small bid.

CRISPIN (*shaking his head*). We met in Eastbourne. Her name was Marigold. . . .

JANE. Eastbourne!

BILL. Honestly, Crispin, more of your past emerges . . .

SUSAN. Whatever were you doing in Eastbourne? Don't tell us.

CRISPIN. Why?

SUSAN. It's bound to be something . . . disgusting!

LOUDSPEAKER: PASSENGERS ON FLIGHT FIVE O FOUR WILL PLEASE COLLECT THEIR HAND BAGGAGE AND PASS THROUGH THE CUSTOMS. . . .

CRISPIN. I'd just come down from the University. My father, the late Admiral, had inconsiderately died at Malta leaving me nothing but his collection of oriental butterflies.

BILL. Parents!

CRISPIN. Faded moth-eaten creatures, stuck through with pins. . . .

During the following speech MICHAEL *and* SUSAN *are not listening but are whispering, their heads together.*

All my friends, even the small dim ones with mackintoshes, seemed to have slipped into employment, jobs were kept

CRISPIN. No home. Only a nice independent room in Gloucester Road.

MICHAEL. How's that landlady?

JANE. With the unbelievable name.

CRISPIN. Mrs. Garden-Keeper, the sprightly widow of an Indian Civil Servant? Quite well, and so is her daughter Paddy. Paddy Garden-Keeper . . . (*He laughs.*) Isn't it a wonderful name? As a matter of fact she reminds me a little of the long-lost Mrs. Crispin. I get the same feeling of guilt when she blows her nose. That sad work with the handkerchief!

They laugh.

Show some respect. For the woman I live with!

SUSAN. Crispin, you don't!

CRISPIN. Only in her dreams.

SUSAN. Poor girl! I bet she dreams continually.

CRISPIN. What else can she do? She spent all her early emotional years in jodhpurs and now she's deprived of her horse.

JANE. Why?

CRISPIN. No room in the flat, and the cost of oats has been out of the question since Daddy died. So she sits at home in the evenings, her thoughts full of the triumph of forgotten potato races in long-distant gymkhanas. She closes her eyes and she's a child again, riding round the ring with a rosette clutched between the wired teeth. . . .

He takes a flower from the counter and grips it between his teeth, making cantering motions on his bar stool.

JANE. Can't she find anyone . . . to take the place of the horses?

CRISPIN. There's a boy from the travel agency where she works, but I don't think he's greatly interested. She's not a great pleasure to the eye. . . .

SUSAN (*contemptuously*). Then what can she expect?

CRISPIN. Snob!

SUSAN. What do you mean?

CRISPIN. When you have the social security of that marvellous mouth!

SUSAN (*pleased*). You're ridiculous!

CRISPIN. Spare a thought for the under-privileged.

SUSAN. Like Paddy?

CRISPIN. We spend millions on free walking-sticks, wigs for the bald, and the provision of plastic tobacco pouches for vicars unfrocked through no fault of their own, but what party's committed to seeing that there's a level of basic beauty below which no girl need ever fall?

JANE. Probably the Liberals.

SUSAN. My aunt's a Liberal.

JANE. They must be committed to *something*.

SUSAN. It's guilt . . . you must have a great guilt about her.

CRISPIN. Who?

SUSAN. This Miss Garden-Keeper you keep on about so. . . .

CRISPIN. Guilt? (*He looks at the clock.*)

SUSAN. Why does it make you feel *bad* . . . That she's not Miss Stratosphere of nineteen sixty?

CRISPIN. Well, I suppose . . . (*He is a little ashamed.*) Last night words galloped away with me.

JANE. They always do.

MICHAEL. Crispin! What *have* you been saying now?

CRISPIN. I said it more to fill in one of those gaps in the conversation . . .

JANE. Those gaps!

CRISPIN. Those long black pauses which are such a feature of life within the Garden-Keepers in Gloucester Road.

JANE. So you had to rush in? . . .

CRISPIN. Imagine it! A cold wet Thursday night and I was kept from meeting my friends by the embarrassing lack of

whom I was once at college. Oh, in the year dot! He had a job in the Home Office and had been searching for me for some time to see if I could lecture on the surrealist movement to the inmates of Wormwood Scrubs . . . I had to rush straight out and find his whisky in his fine Georgian mansion in Belsize Park. It was late after we'd finished talking, and Mrs. Henshaw made me uncomfortable on the Chippendale in their draughty great downstairs. In the morning Henshaw gave me a small sum of money, provided I promised not to lecture . . . He said my memories of the Left Bank would lead the prisoners to mutiny. I haven't been back since. No moment to speak to Paddy . . . but as I went out of the door . . .

BILL. What?

CRISPIN. It seemed we had . . . reached an understanding.

Pause. Then he says, reassuring himself:

I'm quite safe. She won't come.

JANE. Why not?

CRISPIN. It'll be a thought, an idea for her to treasure. Like an old pony club rosette. Pressed between the pages of her *Horse and Hound Annual Year Book*. Something for her to take out and sigh over occasionally . . . But (*Again persuading himself.*) she'll never come. . . .

SUSAN. He's right, of course . . . He knows her character.

CRISPIN. If she was the sort of girl to come, would she be the sort of girl to be stuck with Mummy in a small maisonette and nothing but a distant gaze at the young man across the travel folders to brighten up her dark days at the railway bookings counter?

JANE. Well, if I was her . . .

BILL. You're not. Thank God!

JANE. I believe I'd seize the opportunity . . .

CRISPIN. Opportunities are things she's never seized.

MICHAEL. The world's passed her by?

CRISPIN. Ever since she dismounted for the last time. So although she may toy with the idea she'll never act on it.

SUSAN. Rather sad!

CRISPIN. And we'll never refer to it again. She'll sidle past me on the stairs, her eyes turned away, and I'll smile and she'll think I was all ready, tonight, to take her to Paris.

SUSAN. Crispin . . . You're not!

JANE. The deception!

CRISPIN. Not at all. I asked her to come and she didn't. She deceived *me* not turning up like that. After all, it isn't every day I ask a girl to fly to Paris.

JANE. She's let you down?

CRISPIN. We can honestly say so.

Pause.

It's another of those events that haven't happened, like the flights we go on each evening, to distant parts of the globe.

LOUDSPEAKER: WE ANNOUNCE THE DEPARTURE OF FLIGHT FIVE O NINE TO VANCOUVER.

SUSAN. You sound regretful.

CRISPIN. I'd as soon be flying on that frozen trip to Canada as dashing through the air with Paddy. There's nothing to worry about. *We're grounded!*

JANE. You're safe!

CRISPIN. And the aeroplane, as it always does, can leave without us. . . .

He is about to drink coffee when his eyes become fixed and riveted with horror at something he can see off stage. He slowly puts the coffee cup down. Then he turns towards the bar and buries his face in his hands.

MICHAEL. What is it?

SUSAN. Is he ill?

JANE. The wet . . . shoes.

CRISPIN. It's not the shoes. (*In a terrible whisper.*) It's Miss Garden-Keeper. Equipped with luggage!

> PADDY GARDEN-KEEPER, *carrying a suitcase and dressed for travel, enters slowly. She sits at the opposite end of the coffee bar from the group round* CRISPIN *and does not look at him.* LIZ *comes up to her behind the bar, and* PADDY *orders a cup of coffee.*
> *When it is brought,* PADDY *takes out a handkerchief and thoroughly blows her nose. With a look of doom* CRISPIN *leaves his friends and approaches* PADDY. *He sits on a stool beside her. While* CRISPIN *talks to* PADDY *his friends talk, occasionally laughing and whispering together, staring at* CRISPIN *to see how he is getting on from time to time.*

CRISPIN. Hullo.
PADDY (*as if surprised*). Oh. Hullo.

> *She has a scrubbed appearance and a nervous, Kensington accent. Her clothes are shabby and her shoes need repairing. Her ankles are thick and her nose shines in the hard neon light of the waiting-room.*

CRISPIN. Surprised to see me?
PADDY. Yes. Rather . . .
CRISPIN. You didn't think I'd be here?
PADDY (*she giggles,* CRISPIN *winces*). Well, not really.

> *He sits down beside her on a stool.*

CRISPIN. You couldn't have thought I'd be so heartless . . . as not to come at all?
PADDY. I know you're not heartless.
CRISPIN. I hope you go on thinking that!
PADDY. Why?
CRISPIN (*taking breath*). Miss Garden-Keeper . . . (*He nerves himself for what he has to say.*) I've got to tell you . . .

I know this sounds terrible, but I'm not here for the reason you think. In fact, I . . .

LOUDSPEAKER (*booming*): WILL MR. EVERARD PLEASE COME TO THE INQUIRY DESK. MR. EVERARD TO THE INQUIRY DESK. MR. EVERARD TO THE INQUIRY DESK. PLEASE.

PADDY (*sneezing*). Sorry. What did you say?

CRISPIN (*deflated*). You've got a cold.

PADDY. Yes.

CRISPIN. You should be in bed. Nursing it, you know. I mean, looking at you I can see quite clearly you're in no condition to travel.

PADDY. I'll be all right!

CRISPIN. Paris is draughty, at this time of year . . . Those wide streets—you can stand by the Louvre and feel the cold wind all the way from the Arc de Triomphe. . . .

She opens her case, brings out a guide book and starts searching on a map.

What's that?

PADDY. I'm looking for it. . . .

CRISPIN. What?

PADDY. The Arc de Triomphe.

Miserably he points it out.

CRISPIN. Here. . . .

PADDY. I bought this today.

CRISPIN. I hope it wasn't expensive.

PADDY (*looking at her book*). It must be marvellous . . . the vistas . . .

CRISPIN. Vistas . . . Oh, they're not very much. I mean, personally, give me Hyde Park Corner. . . .

PADDY. You don't mean that. . . .

CRISPIN. I definitely do . . . And in Paris they have this low creeping sort of mist. Very treacherous. With a cold coming on.

PADDY. I've got this muffler.

She pulls a big school muffler across her face.

CRISPIN. I see you have.

PADDY. You see, I'm all equipped. Even down to phrases.

She brings another small book out of her case and reads a phrase: "J'ai une douleur ici dans la poitrine."

CRISPIN. I don't suppose you'll need that really. . . .

PADDY. I wish I'd learnt more. When I was meant to be at my French Prep I was always volunteering to muck out the stables.

CRISPIN *winces.*

PADDY. Silly, really. Now I haven't got a pony, but I *am* going to Paris.

CRISPIN. I . . . shouldn't be too sure.

PADDY. What do you mean?

CRISPIN (*desperately*). Weather conditions! On my way out here I thought . . . fog was about to fall.

LOUDSPEAKER: WE NOW ANNOUNCE THE FLIGHT OF OUR NUMBER NINE O NINE TO HAMBURG AND BERLIN. WILL PASSENGERS PLEASE PASS THROUGH THE CUSTOMS AT CHANNEL FOUR.

PADDY. They *are* flying.

CRISPIN (*looking at her*). And you're excited?

PADDY (*entranced*). I don't feel asleep!

CRISPIN. I see.

LIZ (*coming up the bar*). Coffee, dear?

CRISPIN. Have another coffee?

PADDY. It seems so long waiting.

CRISPIN. You don't know . . . how long it can be. (*He fumbles in his pockets.*) . . . Have you got any change?

PADDY (*looking at him but not in her bag*). No. I haven't.

She seems, as she says this, drugged with happiness and remote.

CRISPIN. Excuse me. . . .

He goes back along the bar to the group of his friends. They begin to question him eagerly:

SUSAN. Did you tell her?

MICHAEL. We waited for the tears. . . .

JANE. The screams of rage.

SUSAN. A woman scorned . . . And attacking you with a plastic butter-knife.

CRISPIN. Two bob.

MICHAEL. What?

CRISPIN. Lend it me for the coffee.

SUSAN (*accusingly*). *You haven't told her yet!*

CRISPIN. Well, it's not easy! You can't just blurt out, "I didn't mean it. Go home to your mother. We're not going anywhere." You can't just drop a bomb on her like that!

JANE. You're slipping! Where's that ruthless approach?

SUSAN. Of the man who walked out of marriage owing to the shape of the supper plates!

CRISPIN. Good heavens! I'm not getting involved. I'm not *taking* her anywhere . . . It just requires . . . a little *finesse*! That's all it just requires. And two bob!

He takes it quickly from a pile of money BILL *is playing with on the counter, and goes back to* PADDY. *He sits beside her and they drink coffee.*
Pause.

Those are my friends. . . .

PADDY. Oh, yes?

CRISPIN. You may think they look rather young. . . .

PADDY (*looking at them*). The girls seem to be dressed . . . for the Polar Regions.

CRISPIN. Oh, they're not going anywhere.

PADDY (*frowning*). What're they doing here, then?

CRISPIN. Well, they come here every night!

PADDY. What for?

CRISPIN. They don't believe in travel. They just come here for the sake of coming. . . .

PADDY. *I think that's ridiculous.*

CRISPIN. Can't you understand . . . the charm of not travelling. . . .

PADDY. Just . . . sitting here?

CRISPIN. Yes . . . Listening to the announcements, the strange foreign voices.

PADDY. I'd like to hear those foreign voices at closer quarters!

CRISPIN. Look! Go to a bullfight in Seville and shut your eyes and you might just as well not have moved out of . . . Selfridges! Lie on the beach at Capri, and hear the pale typists in their tall flowerpot hats and too many necklaces discuss the weather in Manchester. Mount the Champs Elysées . . .

PADDY (*looking at her guide book*). Where's that?

CRISPIN (*pointing*). There . . . for a jolly good British breakfast and meat-tea snack.

PADDY (*entranced and looking at him*). Can you?

CRISPIN (*thundering on regardless*). But stay here, just here, for a strong feeling of strangeness and the low meaningless murmur of love . . . LOOK!

> CRISPIN *nods to where, down the bar,* BILL *and* JANE, *and* MICHAEL *and* SUSAN *are whispering in pairs.*

PADDY. I've never been abroad!

CRISPIN. Preserve your illusions intact!

PADDY. How do you mean?

CRISPIN. Shut your eyes.

> *She shuts them.* CRISPIN *goes on, in a soft voice:*

You're in a gondola, floating through the warm velvet night down the *Canal Grande*. (*He gives it the full Italian pronunciation*, Canal Grand—ay.)

PADDY. Am I?

> MISS GARDEN-KEEPER'S *eyes are shut.* LIZ, *passing down the bar with a wet cloth to wipe it, looks at her with surprise.*

CRISPIN. The gondolier gives his little warning cry as you come round the corner of a crumbling palace. "Owl!" Then he sings. . . .
(*Singing.*) *Santa Lucia* . . .
　　　　　Santa . . . *Lu* . . . *ci—ah!*
Enjoying the holiday?

PADDY (*thoughtfully*). Mmm, yes. I suppose so.

CRISPIN. But if we were really on that Grand Canal we'd be in a constant state of anxiety about the pound a minute the small craft was liable to be costing. Your dinner would no doubt have been an unappetizing fish sliced into hard rubber teething rings which would be sitting uneasily on your stomach. Mosquitoes would be dive-bombing your unprotected extremities. . . .

PADDY (*opening her eyes*). Oh!

CRISPIN. I should be tipping the boat to feel in my pocket in case the travellers' cheques had been extracted by some pool-eyed child on the Bridge of Sighs, and we should both be longing for the safe, cheap top of a bright red bus.

PADDY. We should?

CRISPIN. That is, if we'd both set out together.

PADDY. But we're not going to Venice. . . .

CRISPIN. Thank God for it!

PADDY. Paris!

CRISPIN. It's the same.

PADDY. I get the feeling that you don't want me to leave the country.

CRISPIN. You see! You hardly know me. . . .

PADDY. I know you quite well.

CRISPIN. You've seen me on your home ground . . . that comfortable little apartment with its fine framed photographs of the various horses in your life!

PADDY. You cheer Mummy up. She's always said so.

CRISPIN. I add colour to your lives?

PADDY. When you wear that big tweed overcoat Mummy says you remind her of—Ronald Coleman.

CRISPIN. Who?

PADDY. Apparently he was a film star. Sort of years ago. I believe she's fallen.

CRISPIN. Who?

PADDY. Mummy.

CRISPIN. Well, at one time your mother must have been quite an attractive woman. . . .

PADDY. In India Daddy had all sorts of trouble with her.

CRISPIN. That's where you were born? . . .

PADDY. I was a child. I remember running away from my nurse and picking up a lot of little bright red seeds. They sent me home when I was twelve, because of the climate bringing me on too suddenly.

CRISPIN. They got you back in time?

PADDY (laughing). Don't worry.

CRISPIN. But I'm trying to tell you . . .

PADDY. What?

CRISPIN. Perhaps I amuse you, provide a breath of fresh air. Something different from your life at the pony club. Something that you don't meet among the workers at the travel agency, or your mother doesn't encounter cramming little black cocktail dresses all day on intractable females with the outsize look.

PADDY (thoughtfully). No. . . .

CRISPIN (taking no notice of her). But get me abroad and how my character might change! Give a man a passport and a limited amount of currency and new sides emerge. He becomes very mean, and continually takes you out for lunch which is no more than a shared portion of *pommes frites*. Or he becomes very truculent and creates embarrassing scenes with taxi drivers which lead to the intervention of the police. Or a great interest in love revives in him. He drags you to ruinous night clubs where the undressed girls quiver and glow like tall white fish in an aquarium. And in the end he makes contact with a visiting Swede and leaves you with the bill unpaid in a high, unheated bedroom with a poor view of the Gare du Nord.

PADDY. I wouldn't worry you'd turn out like that.

CRISPIN (*disappointed*). You wouldn't?

PADDY. I think you'd stay with anyone. . . .

CRISPIN. Whatever makes you think that?

PADDY. Mummy worries about you, of course.

CRISPIN. She does?

PADDY. She wonders how any man can make do on one pair of shoes.

CRISPIN (*looking at them*). These shoes!

PADDY. But I didn't worry about you until . . .

CRISPIN. Until what?

PADDY. I saw your friends were all young people.

CRISPIN. But I cultivate that fresh, new generation!

PADDY (*looking at the clock*). The time creeps on slowly!

CRISPIN. But it's time for me definitely to tell you . . .

PADDY. Why are all your friends as *young* as that?

CRISPIN. You don't like them?

PADDY. I've never been introduced.

CRISPIN. They're young. They look splendidly well, and I can't tell you the weekly wages their parents pass into their indifferent hands by way of pocket money. They're the sort of circle I've always had, at the University.

PADDY. But you've left the University, years ago.

CRISPIN (*disregarding her*). They hold the moment . . . between growing up and dying, which occupies the rest of our years . . . like a pause. Before they pass their exams and get married and start putting down on a little house.

PADDY. *They* do!

> *She looks at them.* MICHAEL *is now carefully balancing a paper cup on his forehead. The others are watching him without rapture.*

CRISPIN. The only years when we see things clearly. When we have the courage of the anarchy within us.

PADDY. I like men . . . a few years older.

CRISPIN. You're flattering me!

PADDY. I didn't mean that. I meant . . . I like them when they start to plan the mortgage. . . .

CRISPIN. Now that is a stage I have to reach. Thinking of the rent's quite enough. (*Hastily.*) Although, your mother's quite safe.

PADDY. Perhaps you cling too hard to those years, Mr. Crispin.

CRISPIN. What?

PADDY. Wouldn't it be more comfortable to mix with friends of your own age?

CRISPIN (*looking at her hard*). That's the way it strikes you?

PADDY. Not that it's my affair.

CRISPIN. You've thought about this.

PADDY. Hardly at all.

CRISPIN. But what you say may show some perception.

PADDY. I just thought I might say it, seeing that you're here.

CRISPIN. Yes. I'm here. I'll tell you this, now we've reached such a high pitch of almost unendurable honesty. I shouldn't be here. I should be at home!

PADDY. Only with older friends, I suggested.

CRISPIN. I should never have said what I've said to you.

PADDY. Oh, don't worry. I expect you have to show off your anarchy or something.

CRISPIN. The things I've said, that'd better be forgotten.

PADDY. And Mummy loves being shocked; that's why she gets those great long books out of the library, about eighteenth-century tarts . . .

CRISPIN. It's time I told you. . . .

PADDY. What?

CRISPIN. That I've deceived you, in a sense.

PADDY. Why?

CRISPIN. For instance, I'm married.

PADDY. Well, so I should have thought!

CRISPIN (*disappointed*). I thought I gave off an air of freedom!

PADDY. You seem too soft-hearted not to have been married at some stage.

CRISPIN. Soft-hearted?

PADDY. I'd say so.

CRISPIN. I tell you. I left my wife quite brutally. Over a matter of side plates!

PADDY. It takes a soft-hearted person to leave anyone in a brutal manner.

CRISPIN. Look . . .

PADDY. Yes?

CRISPIN. Where did you gather up all this curious experience of life?

PADDY. Well, I've met people, since Daddy died of course.

CRISPIN. Then you must realize. I'm not a suitable person for you to get tangled up with!

PADDY. You've been a perfect lodger.

CRISPIN (*furious*). Perfect!

PADDY. And respectable.

CRISPIN (*insulted*). You'll be saying next . . . I'm quiet!

PADDY. Well, much quieter than that bank manager we had before you . . . who gave such noisy parties. Mummy found a girl quite undressed one Sunday afternoon in the kitchen, making toast.

CRISPIN (*appalled*). *A bank manager!*

PADDY. With the North Country Providential.

CRISPIN. Miss Garden-Keeper, don't let's get side-tracked. I'm sorry I'm married.

PADDY. I'm sorry you're sorry.

CRISPIN. For the effect it's had.

PADDY. On me?

CRISPIN. *On your journey.*

PADDY. Well, I can't see why you being married should stop me going to Paris.

CRISPIN. You don't?

PADDY. I'm sorry about it, of course. But you can't expect that sad fact to keep me permanently in England.

CRISPIN. Have you no moral sense?

PADDY. I don't understand.

CRISPIN. Perhaps . . . they didn't get you away from India quickly enough.

> PADDY *laughs.*

But it's no good. My being married is a great barrier. I couldn't face your mother . . .

PADDY. Need she know?

CRISPIN. What?

PADDY. About your marriage?

CRISPIN. She's bound to hear . . . in time. I tell you, I only drifted into it through a gap in the conversation.

PADDY. Oh.

CRISPIN. We were standing on the front at Eastbourne. The French boys of whom I had charge were smoking furtive cigarettes and writing up rude words in the shelter. I'd only known Marigold a week. None of my University friends had written that day, and I was feeling lonely. There seemed nothing for us to talk about . . . the silence was oppressive. So I said "Will you marry me?" For the sake of a remark. Before I knew where I was, she had fallen against me like a felled tree. The French boys were sniggering at us and I was trying to comfort myself by the thought of the small capital I knew she had in the National Savings.

PADDY. You should have been ruthless. . . .

CRISPIN. What?

PADDY. And pretended you'd never spoken.

CRISPIN (*gets up, determined and excited*). You're right! Ruthlessness is the only answer. It's kinder, in the long run.

PADDY. Of course. Cruel to be kind. . . .

CRISPIN. Say what you mean!

PADDY. And don't speak until you mean it!

He takes a deep breath.

CRISPIN. Miss Garden-Keeper . . .

PADDY. Yes.

His mouth moves soundlessly as his words are drowned by an announcement booming from the loud speaker.

LOUDSPEAKER: WE ANNOUNCE THE DEPARTURE OF OUR FLIGHT NUMBER NINE O FOUR FOR ROME, NAPLES AND CYPRUS. WILL PASSENGERS FOR ROME, NAPLES AND CYPRUS PLEASE COLLECT THEIR HAND BAGGAGE AND PROCEED TO THE CUSTOMS ON CHANNEL FIVE IMMEDIATELY.

CRISPIN. Paddy . . .

LOUDSPEAKER: AND WILL MR. EVERARD PLEASE REPORT TO THE INQUIRY DESK. MR. EUSTACE EVERARD TO THE INQUIRY DESK, PLEASE. THANK YOU!

While this announcement has been going on, CRISPIN *has been inaudibly mouthing, and* PADDY *has opened her case again and taken out a hat, elaborate, veiled and trimmed with artificial roses.*

The announcement finishes and CRISPIN *is looking at her with unbearable guilt.*

PADDY. Were you saying something, Mr. Crispin?

CRISPIN. What's that you're putting on?

PADDY (*laughing*). A hat, of course.

CRISPIN (*appalled*). A hat, for Paris!

PADDY. I'm sorry. I wasn't listening. What were you trying to say, Mr. Crispin?

He looks at the hat and sinks down on the bar stool defeated.

CRISPIN. Nothing . . . Miss Garden-Keeper. Hardly anything at all.

Looking at her with guilt and misery, CRISPIN *retreats, back to the company of his friends.* PADDY *is left alone, sitting quietly and wearing her hat.*

SUSAN (*as* CRISPIN *approaches*). What *is* it?

CRISPIN. Her hat. She's bought it specially.

JANE. For Paris.

MICHAEL. The Bois de Boulogne.

CRISPIN. I can't look. Those angry roses glare at me accusingly.

JANE. That does make it difficult for you, I do see.

CRISPIN. Impossible!

MICHAEL. Come on, Crispin!

BILL. Be a bit ruthless.

CRISPIN. But I'm not a murderer, am I? Don't credit me with that.

SUSAN. What do you mean?

CRISPIN. I just can't say "Take that thing off your head and pack it away", when it represents weeks of overtime with the *Railway Guide* and God knows how many nights of dreaming.

Pause.

JANE. There's only one way out!

CRISPIN. What?

JANE. One decent way of keeping the hat on her head and the smile on her face.

CRISPIN. What is it?

JANE. You'll have to take her.

MICHAEL. It's absurd!

BILL. How can he?

SUSAN. He can't go *that* far.

MICHAEL. With *that* girl. Of all the girls in the world.

JANE. Well, why not?

MICHAEL. She simply . . . isn't Crispin's type of female company.

JANE. He's not going to *marry* her. Just fly her across the Channel!

CRISPIN (*thinking of Paris, entranced for a moment*). The Metro smelling like wet tin, the onion soup by the meat market! (*Then he shakes his head.*) It's impossible. (*He looks at the clock.*) There isn't much time, to explain that hat off her head.

JANE. You'll have to go!

CRISPIN (*doubtfully*). And explain afterwards, that I never seriously meant to take her.

JANE. Why explain?

CRISPIN. I'll have to some time. It's absurd! (*He pauses, then says.*) You have to do something ridiculous from time to time.

BILL. He's going!

JANE. He's got to!

CRISPIN. Paris! I'll hardly remember the way to the Café Flore. And when I get there, they'll ask me to pay for the pile of saucers I crept away from in 1939.

BILL. They may have forgotten.

CRISPIN. They've got long memories . . . the French. I can't go. Possibly.

JANE. Why not?

CRISPIN. Be practical . . . I've got . . . (*He feels in his pockets.*) Nothing at all!

JANE. We'll start a collection.

BILL. For Crispin's journey.

SUSAN. We'll float a loan. . . .

MICHAEL. A loan for the love of Allah. . . .

> *He limps with his cap.* CRISPIN *stops him in case* PADDY *should notice: but in fact she is sitting imperturbable in her hat, not regarding them.*

SUSAN (*with pity*). Look at her. Think what you'd be conferring on her!

CRISPIN. A favour? Yes. (*Self-satisfied.*) It'd be a great favour, there's no doubt about that.

SUSAN. I mean . . . it's probably the only time she'll have that sort of adventure. . . .

CRISPIN. Certainly, the only time. What a thing to look back on. A spell with me, across the Channel! What a memory . . . For the long future in Gloucester Road!

BILL. Perhaps she's got some money?

CRISPIN. You mean . . . go Dutch? (*Pause.*) She must expect to pay. Well, we all have to pay for experience!

> PADDY *is now reading her ticket, which she has taken out of her bag.* CRISPIN *approaches her, leaving his watching friends.*

You're reading your ticket. . . .

> *She puts it away, as if caught in some absurdity.*

Well, it passes the time. And it's always as well, when you're going anywhere, to make sure you haven't got a ticket for somewhere else entirely.

PADDY. The agency gave it me, at a reduction.

> *Pause.*

CRISPIN. Of course. Just one, they gave you?

PADDY. Yes.

CRISPIN. And you've got the odd scrap of currency, in case your eye lights on something in the Dior *boutique*.

She takes out a ten thousand franc note.

A great table-cloth of money that'd hardly press you a duck on the Eiffel Tower . . . still, it might last a couple of days, if you can keep going on omelettes.

PADDY. You want to know a lot about my financial arrangements.

CRISPIN. Only what you've got set aside, in case you're stranded.

PADDY. Am I?

CRISPIN. What?

PADDY. Going to be stranded?

CRISPIN. I know in the old days it wasn't thought right to ask a lady what she had in her purse before she went anywhere, but we live in a Modern Age.

PADDY. Do we?

CRISPIN. The sexes having become equal.

PADDY. Equal?

CRISPIN. You don't feel it?

PADDY. I like a man to offer me everything . . . on a great impulse.

CRISPIN (*understandingly*). The meal ordered, followed by a swift dive through the window of the gents when the bill comes to be presented?

PADDY (*laughs*). I wouldn't like *that*.

CRISPIN. But it's the thought that counts.

PADDY. Backed up by a little financial goodwill.

CRISPIN. Excuse me a moment. . . .

PADDY. You're going away again?

CRISPIN. Only to say goodbye. To my friends.

PADDY. Oh . . . to *them*.

CRISPIN. I'll be back.

Pause.

L.H.—E

Don't you trust me, Miss Garden-Keeper?

PADDY. Trust you? I don't know that I've thought about it.

CRISPIN (*looking at her, moved*). Such faith!

> *He makes off towards his friends. As he rejoins the group he says:*

Really, it's moving. . . .

BILL. What is?

CRISPIN. Such faith. In my genuine offer.

JANE. It's only become genuine in the course of the last ten minutes.

CRISPIN. She believes in me intensely. Whatever happens will never spoil the deep reality of this moment.

JANE. Except your slight lack of funds.

CRISPIN. What a worldly little creature you've become, with the approach of matrimony.

SUSAN. All that touching faith won't pay for your week-end.

MICHAEL. Here. Look what we've collected.

> *He hands* CRISPIN *money.*

CRISPIN (*counting*).   Three . . . four . . . five . . . five. Six. And such clean English money. How can you have so much?

JANE. We joined together. For the cause.

MICHAEL. The greatest joke in the history of London Airport!

CRISPIN (*putting the money away quickly*). No! Don't mock it, please. Don't do that. There's a faith over there under that nodding vegetation, which mustn't ever be shattered. How much is a ticket?

JANE (*picking up a brochure*). Paris. Nine pounds nineteen. Night flight.

CRISPIN. Another four in ten minutes . . . it should be possible.

JANE. And what are you going to do when you get there? Drive straight to the nearest doss-house?

CRISPIN (*dreaming*). To the Hotel de la Grande Armée. Third on the right off the Boulevard Montparnasse. Full of brass bedsteads and portable radios and the strong, protective smell of soup. Where they keep the bath taps under lock and key and let your room if you're out for five minutes in the afternoon.

BILL. But the money. . . .

CRISPIN. You know what they are at the Hotel de la Grande Armée? Light fingered! Their palms itch. They can extract the electric razor from an American Action Painter before he's got his baggage unzipped. So when we've been there a couple of hours I slap my pocket in horror and discover . . .

SUSAN. What?

CRISPIN. That the honour of France is stained with another great crime against humanity . . . and someone's knocked off my wallet!

JANE. That you didn't have?

CRISPIN. The illusion will be maintained. The great faith'll be unbroken. And from then on we'll go Dutch on Miss Garden-Keeper's ten thousand francs. Well, it's a small price to pay, for a week-end she'll have all her life to remember. And the sky tonight . . . looks like an invitation!

Pause.

MICHAEL. What is it?

CRISPIN. An idea! Just a moment! Thank God I'm still creative!

He leaves them and goes hurriedly off. SUSAN *looks along the bar at* PADDY, *who has ordered another coffee and is working on her French phrases.*

MICHAEL. He's crazy. . . .

SUSAN. He's going to take her! If only she knew . . .

MICHAEL. She'll think he's mad for her.

BILL. It must be wonderful . . . to be his age. And still go on doing such crazy things!

JANE (*looking at him sceptically*). Must it?

BILL (*determined*). Well, yes. I hope I never get dull.

JANE. If I didn't think you were going to get dull . . .

BILL. What?

JANE. I'd leave you. Tomorrow!

> CRISPIN *returns with the* SWEEPER *and talks to him confidentially in a corner down stage.*

CRISPIN. I'm offering you a great opportunity. . . .

SWEEPER. What?

CRISPIN (*taking off his overcoat*). This. At a positively knock-down price. A fine great bit of tweed in which I've often slept and made love and . . .

SWEEPER. You want to sell it. (*He feels it.*)

CRISPIN. Was once used to smuggle a small Sinhalese dancer into the University Debating Society disguised as the late Professor Joad on a certain memorable occasion! It's a garment . . . with history!

SWEEPER. Why do you want to flog it?

CRISPIN. I tell you . . . there's a great enterprise afoot!

SWEEPER. A what?

CRISPIN. I'm going abroad. . . .

SWEEPER (*incredulous*). You!

CRISPIN. I'm taking to the air . . . tonight. When you're sweeping up these old coffee cups and *Evening Standards*, I'll be up in the sky above you! Don't you envy me?

SWEEPER. No!

CRISPIN. Not at all? I'm asking five pounds for the coat.

SWEEPER. There's a bit of weight to this coat. Sort of country gentleman style, it could be termed. . . .

CRISPIN. Wear it at point to points. Come on. I need the money.

SWEEPER. I'm not a great lover of abroad. . . .

CRISPIN. Whyever not?

SWEEPER. Four pounds ten. It's the dogs. . . .

CRISPIN. The dogs?

SWEEPER. Say four pounds.

CRISPIN. What worries you about the dogs?

SWEEPER. If you get bitten in any part of the United Kingdom it's a more or less trivial occurrence. But abroad . . .

CRISPIN. Well?

SWEEPER. You've got to drop whatever you may be doing and have an immediate injection! Rabies . . . It's not safe . . . Not to be bitten by them foreign dogs! Make it three pound ten.

CRISPIN. Quick then. I can't haggle with you any more. . . .

He takes money from the SWEEPER *and gives him the coat. As he runs off stage he says:*

Insular. That's what you are!

As he runs he jumps triumphantly and gives a small dog-like howl. The SWEEPER, *holding the coat, looks after him and then goes.*

A FEMALE AMERICAN TOURIST *enters and looks round behind her.* CRISPIN *is following her, carrying her luggage.*

CRISPIN. And when you get into London, ma'am, *please* don't forget the Soane Museum. The Hogarths have such strength!

TOURIST (*looking in her purse*). Porter, how much is it customary to tip porters here? I'm not used to your currency.

CRISPIN (*as they disappear*). Not more than two pounds. Don't be taken advantage of.

They go.

SUSAN (*looking after them*). What's he up to now?

MICHAEL. *Something.*

SUSAN. You can trust Crispin to do something extraordinary.

BILL. I don't believe he'll manage it, though.

JANE (*looking at* PADDY). She'll be stood up. You ever been stood up, Susan.

SUSAN. No. But I've stood plenty of people.

JANE. It must be *ghastly*.

MICHAEL. She's probably used to it.

> CRISPIN *enters waving a ticket in one hand, his other raised in a salute of victory. He goes smiling up to* PADDY.

JANE. He's got it!

MICHAEL. You see . . . something extraordinary. . . .

SUSAN. What do we do now?

BILL. We go quietly . . . and leave the rest to history. What a story he'll have to tell . . . in the pub on Monday.

JANE. I hope it's a happy story.

BILL. It'll be hilarious!

JANE (*putting her arm in his*). Come on. We've really got to stop watching them now!

> *The young people,* SUSAN, MICHAEL, BILL *and* JANE, *leave with elaborate stealth.*

CRISPIN. I've managed it!

PADDY. What, Mr. Crispin?

CRISPIN. Something you mustn't know about—oh, in the years to come, perhaps. But now, you can still trust me.

PADDY. Robert!

> CRISPIN *turns round. A young man of great respectability named* MR. ROBERT WALSH *has entered and joined them. He is carrying a mackintosh and luggage.*

MR. WALSH. I had to explain it all to Frank. And get away from the parents. Did you worry?

PADDY. Terribly. But I had Mr. Crispin to keep me entertained. He kept coming backwards and forwards.

CRISPIN. Mr. . . .

PADDY. Walsh. He works at our agency. We're . . . friendly.

CRISPIN. I see.

PADDY. And this is Mr. Crispin. My mother's P.G.

MR. WALSH. Pleased to meet you. (*He nods at* CRISPIN *nervously*.) I'll get some reading matter, darling. For the air.

PADDY. Don't be long! (*As he goes to the bookstall off stage, she looks after him with love.*) It's almost time. . . .

PADDY *and* CRISPIN *are left together.*

(*anxiously*). Mr. Crispin. You won't tell Mummy?

CRISPIN. No. . . .

PADDY. She's the sort that only likes love in library books.

CRISPIN. I won't tell her.

PADDY. And Robert's parents don't really know. He lives near here. In Staines. That's why we came separately. They think he's gone to the pictures.

CRISPIN. Won't they think it's rather . . . a long epic?

PADDY. A friend'll ring them and say he's staying the weekend. His friend, Frank, from the Territorials. He often goes to him, for the week-end.

Pause.

You don't approve. . . .

CRISPIN. It's the deceit.

PADDY. Well, you can't expect to enjoy yourself. Not if you go round telling the truth to everybody.

CRISPIN. You understand that!

PADDY. We've saved up for this, a long time. Robert's worked.

CRISPIN. I've been working too.

PADDY. No? How marvellous. What at?

CRISPIN. Harder, it seems, than ever in my life before. Miss Garden-Keeper . . .

PADDY. Yes, Mr. Crispin.

CRISPIN. I don't suppose you remember. Last night. We

were sitting together and the wireless was on. I made a suggestion.

PADDY. I wasn't listening, I'm afraid.

CRISPIN (*incredulously*). You weren't?

PADDY. With this week-end coming, I had so much to think about. I know you were talking, but when you talk . . . You won't think I'm rude?

CRISPIN. No.

PADDY. It's a nice noise most of the time. Like the music you switch on when you peel the potatoes. I mean, you're not really expected to *listen* to it, are you? I mean, half the time, you don't really expect anyone to pay attention.

CRISPIN. Don't I? I don't suppose I do.

LOUDSPEAKER: PASSENGERS FOR OUR FLIGHT NUMBER THREE O SIX TO PARIS PLEASE COLLECT THEIR HAND BAGGAGE AND PROCEED DOWN CHANNEL FIVE FOR PASSPORTS AND CUSTOMS. FLIGHT NUMBER THREE O SIX TO PARIS.

MR. WALSH (*approaching them*). Come on, darling. That's us.

PADDY. Goodbye, Mr. Crispin. You won't . . . tell anyone, our secret?

CRISPIN. No.

They are going, hand in hand, to Channel Five. CRISPIN *looks towards the empty bar stools and sees that his friends, also, have gone.*

Not even . . . you.

The bar is suddenly a big space, almost empty. CRISPIN *walks across the big floor. Then he puts his hands in his pocket and jingles money. On an impulse he goes to a call box and dials a number.*

CRISPIN *telephones.*

Hallo. Is that you? I woke you up? I'm sorry . . . I'm sorry to hear that, Marigold. No, I'm not . . . Really, not at all. Nothing's passed my lips the whole evening . . . except coffee. Purely coffee. Well, when I saw you I said I'd be in touch. I know it was some time last year. But here I am, Marigold. Ringing you again. You see. I keep my promises. I've got a ticket here . . . An air ticket. No . . . perfectly sober, but I wondered if you might care for a holiday. We could sort of . . . share expenses. Paris. It's in France, Marigold . . . from what I can remember . . . a place of great gaiety! Yes . . . Yes . . . I know you're busy. Well, I'm sorry about that time. I didn't know you were serving teas at that hour. I thought they were your friends who might appreciate a drop of something stronger in their cups on that cold day. I was trying to be friendly and hospitable. To join in, Marigold. That's all I was doing. Joining in. Look. Don't hang up. Why don't I come round? For a talk perhaps? There seems to be—no one to talk to. I needn't even stay long. Just—talk a little. Of . . . course. I see. You're tired. Worn out? And a cold coming? All right. All right, Marigold. I'll leave you alone. Entirely alone. I understand. Good night, Marigold.

He puts the telephone back gently, as if not to wake her. He steps out of the call box into the empty bar. He looks for a cigarette in an empty packet and then up to the loudspeaker as it says:

LOUDSPEAKER: THIS IS OUR LAST ANNOUNCEMENT FOR THE MIDNIGHT FLIGHT TO PARIS. WILL PASSENGERS TO PARIS PLEASE PASS THROUGH CHANNEL FIVE. COLLECT YOUR HAND BAGGAGE AND PASS THROUGH CHANNEL FIVE NOW, PLEASE.

Curtain

Two Plays for Television

I have written before of the advantages of writing for television, a pursuit which can be compared to building sand castles below the tide line, or studying the habits of those insects whose life lasts no more than a day. These two plays were long rehearsed, very well performed for a flickering moment, and then vanished. The fact that in that moment they, like other plays on television, were watched by a larger audience than saw all of Shakespeare's plays in his lifetime, is not a helpful or even an encouraging fact to remember.

However, given this death wish for a work of art, television has great advantages. It is a free and relaxed medium for a writer, and while a television play dies quickly, it is not subject to those periods of convalescence and relapse, the continual anxiety of how we did at the Thursday matinée, which are such a tedious and exhausting part of life in the theatre. And I hope that these plays, which were a pleasure to write, may be enjoyable to read. The scripts were written with a minimum of technical terms, what there were have now been removed, and they might be read as long short stories, without all the "She murmured gratefully" or "He muttered, lighting a cigarette" which are the necessary fill-ins for the writer of prose fiction. Perhaps they could even be read aloud, on winter nights, before a defunct television set, or beside one of those on which the wonders of science produce no more than a light pattern of herringbone tweed.

Everyone has his own legend: his private monster and giant. One of mine was the boxing instructor at the school where I went at the age of seven. Boxing seems to me a stupid and ugly occupation for adults; imposed on children, it is obscene and degrading. We had large gloves lashed to the end of our match-stick arms, and were solemnly ordered to fight each other in the full-sized ring of the Chelsea Barracks. Great sergeants with sponges acted, as I remember, as our seconds. I remained terrified of the instructor until I went, with a school friend, to see *Dracula* at a local cinema. We sat watching closely as the Count, in full evening dress, emerged from his coffin to embark on a happy evening with the big toe of one of his sleeping female guests. In our innocence we laughed at this spectacle, but suddenly became conscious of a trembling, heaving, weeping man in the front row—our boxing instructor, convulsed with fear. From that day my terror of him faded, but the idea of the conflict of various sorts of fear remained until I had the chance of writing *David and Broccoli*. Childhood, the most merciless and clearsighted period of our lives, has been neglected in dramatic writing. Hardly anyone is an uninteresting child.

J.M.

David and Broccoli

DAVID AND BROCCOLI was first produced on BBC Television on 26 January 1960, with the following cast:

BROCCOLI	*Esmond Knight*
DAVID	*Diarmid Cammell*
HEADMASTER	*George Benson*
HEADMASTER'S WIFE	*Hazel Hughes*
MINNIE	*Rita Webb*
MR. GOLANSKY	*Peter Sallis*
BOILERMAN	*Toke Townley*
BISHOP	*Charles Weston*

Produced by Michael Elliott

1. The Gymnasium: A large and dreary hall at St. Alfred's Day School for Boys, London, N.W.6. The hall is also used as an Assembly Room, and has a platform with a harmonium on it at one end. Otherwise, ropes climb to the ceiling, there is a vaulting-horse, and the walls are covered with old school photographs. As we fade in the enormous face of BROCCOLI SMITH *fills the screen: broken nose, cauliflower ears and a look of low cunning. He has an expanse of barrel-like chest in a singlet on which the Lilliputian blows of* SMALL BOYS *in boxing gloves patter.*

BROCCOLI. 'It me! Come on you primroses, 'it me. What do you think you're doing? Patting cakes? It's like flies landing. 'It me, you daisy chains. . . .

> *A number of* SMALL BOYS *are queueing up to hit the boxing instructor, who is enthroned upon a chair. One of them, an under-sized boy in glasses, has a tube of sweets with which he is buying his way backwards in the queue. He is* DAVID GOLANSKY.

Know what my old Dad used to do? Put a penny under my pillow, remove it when I was asleep and bash me in the morning because I'd lost it!

> *Obedient titters from the* BOYS.

Strike me, Jackson! 'Arder! Can't you hit 'arder than that, you precious peonies? Again! Bend the arms, Waddilove. You're boxing, not pushing out the old love-cart on Sundays. Not taking a walk with wife and perambulator!

> *Laughter from the* BOYS.

(*He grunts.*) That's better. Rattle my few remaining teeth, Armitage! See if you can make my teeth rattle!

DAVID, *the last in line, is standing in front of him, his hands dangling at his sides.*

Strike me, Golansky!

DAVID, *like a rabbit with a snake, is rooted trembling before the seated boxer.*

(*In a frightful whisper.*) 'It me! Do me a . . . terrible mischief! (*He shouts.*) 'It me, will you?

DAVID (*quietly*). No!

BROCCOLI (*roars*). What?

DAVID (*whispers*). No thank you.

A terrible pause. In the silence the BOYS *are all looking at* DAVID.

BROCCOLI. Per . . . lite!

The BOYS *begin to giggle. Their laughter increases during the following speech and becomes loud and sycophantic. Their faces loom large and laughing around* DAVID. BROCCOLI *is triumphant with his success.*

'It me! You girl guide's delight. Never mind the if you please and thank you. How'd you think I got on in the ring, matched with that Dutch Martin? What did I say . . . Excuse me and *do* you mind? Whilst I was asking his permission I'd have been knocked into the middle of August Bank Holiday . . . Or the Battling Butcher of Amsterdam! When we went twenty rounds in 1923, West Ham Stadium. What do you think we was doing . . . teaching each other nice etiquette?

The BOYS *laugh.*

DAVID (*whispers*). No, Mr. Smith.

BROCCOLI. Mr. Smith! Call me by my nickname, what the boys all use! *The sign of popularity!*

DAVID (*very faint*). Broccoli!

BOYS. Good old Broccoli! Come on, Broccoli! Show him, Broccoli!

BROCCOLI. All right. You hear that? My supporters! 'Undreds of them. Slept out all night for tickets. Roaring themselves 'oarse! Now I'm looming up on you. Looming up terrible . . . Come on. Hate me a little, can't you? Practise your hate on me! 'IT ME!

DAVID (*his voice suddenly loud and uncontrolled*). I CAN'T!

Long pause.

BROCCOLI (*softly*). You non-co-operate with Broccoli and I'll non-co-operate with you. See what the Headmaster has to say!

The BOYS *look appalled and murmur "Headmaster," etc. The bell rings.*

You lot will strike me again next Thursday. Keenly looking forward to it?

BOYS. Yes, Broccoli. Thank you, Broccoli. Goodbye, Broccoli.

They crowd out of the gym.

2. The Changing-Room: The BOYS *are changing, talking and chattering to each other.* DAVID *is a little apart. The* BOYS *aren't speaking to him.* BROCCOLI *passes through the room, putting on his coat.*

He passes near DAVID, *who shrinks against the coats.* BROCCOLI *doesn't notice him. He is passing a window and as the sunlight falls on him, he blinks and rubs his eyes.*

Then he walks on and out. The BOYS *around* DAVID *look admiringly at the retreating* BROCCOLI *and discuss him, a conversation from which* DAVID *is excluded.*

1ST BOY. He was West Ham champion. . . .

4TH BOY. England!

2ND BOY. The world!

L.H.—F

3RD BOY. The Universe!

1ST BOY. Outer Space!

4TH BOY. It's got it on that belt he wears at the end of term . . .

1ST BOY. Bashing Broccoli . . .

3RD BOY. He told us about Dutch Martin . . .

1ST BOY. WE know . . .

3RD BOY. Twenty-five rounds . . .

2ND BOY. At the end they were both . . . unconscious!

3RD BOY. But the Dutchman got unconscious first . . .

4TH BOY. He was *more unconscious* than Broccoli.

1ST BOY. Broccoli's never got *quite* unconscious.

4TH BOY. Even when he took on two at once . . .

2ND BOY. At the Queensway Swimming Baths . . .

3RD BOY. For a gentlemen's wager! . . .

> 1ST BOY *offers round chewing gum. All the boys take one, but when the packet is offered to* DAVID *and he puts out his hand, the* BOY *quickly withdraws the packet.*

1ST BOY. Say "No thank you."

DAVID. Why?

1ST BOY. That's what you are!

DAVID. What?

1ST BOY. A "No thank you."

2ND BOY. Mr. "No thank you very much."

3RD BOY (*bowing elaborately*). No thanks awfully.

1ST BOY (*in an affected posh voice*). Dreadfully sorry, ay'm shoooah!

4TH BOY (*mincing in a wild parody of a classy lady*). Rahlly, ay'm far too fatigued to hit anyone today.

BOYS (*together, laughing*). NO! NO! NO! THANK YOU!

1ST BOY. Mister No Chewing Gum!

4TH BOY (*hissing*). Look out. Broccoli's behind you.

> DAVID *looks round in a panic. No one is there. The laughing,*

jeering BOYS *are all round him. He picks his coat off the peg and runs out of the room and across the passage, jeers ringing behind him.*

3. The Classroom: DAVID *is alone in an empty classroom during break. From the playground outside come noises of games and laughter.* DAVID *sits for a moment, hunched and miserable, on the radiator. Then he goes up on the platform by the blackboard, draws lines and figures on the board, and speaks to the empty desks with calm authority.*

DAVID. Today's briefing is quite simple . . . you men have all been chosen because you are perfectly fit. You have no wives or families and you are all volunteers. This (*He draws.*) is the simple trajectory of our flight . . . We shall head due north until we leave the earth's gravity . . . After that. Well, you're on your own. At about twelve hundred you should feel the pull of Mars. The flight will commence at once. Fasten all seat belts and . . . Good luck!

He goes back to his desk and gets a small model glider out of it. He stands up on the desk and catapults the glider. It sails round the empty classroom and lands on the floor just as the door opens. A BOY *looks in on* DAVID, *still standing on the desk.*

BOY. Golansky! The Headmaster wants to see you.

4. The HEADMASTER'S *room: The* HEADMASTER'S WIFE *is up a ladder, hanging curtains. The* HEADMASTER, *a small alarmed man, smoking a pipe which seems too heavy for his jaw, is looking up at her and passing up tools.*

WIFE. Hammer!

HEADMASTER. Yes, dear.

WIFE. He's not our type . . . not St. Alfred's material.

HEADMASTER. We can't pick and choose, not now we're inspected.

WIFE. Gimlet!

HEADMASTER. Yes, of course. Is *that* it?

WIFE. I understand he lives in an hotel.

HEADMASTER. That may be the trouble. The home background. An hotel, did you say? Oh, dear, yes. That may be
quite the trouble.

WIFE. Pliers!

HEADMASTER. Not here. Shall I get them from your work
bench?

WIFE. Doesn't matter. Now the *screws*!

The door opens and DAVID *sidles in.*

HEADMASTER. Come in, Golansky. My wife's just doing a
little job . . . Quite the man about the house . . . (*He
laughs.*) You don't mind if "Chippy" stays for our chat? . . .

DAVID. No. . . .

HEADMASTER. You see. We know the nicknames you boys
give us. My wife is "Chippy." You call me "Hercules" . . .
no doubt because of my labours!

DAVID. No, I . . .

HEADMASTER. Don't worry, Golansky. Good heavens, it's
only part of the atmosphere and shows the school is a well-
run and happy ship! "Chippy," "Hercules" . . . and our
well-loved professional, Mr. Smith, is "Broccoli," isn't he?
What do they call you?

DAVID. Golansky, sir.

HEADMASTER (*shocked*). Your *real* name?

DAVID (*miserably*). Yes.

HEADMASTER. You see! I'm afraid you haven't quite fitted in
among us yet. Not quite had your . . . corners rubbed off,
shall we say?

DAVID. I didn't want to hit him.

HEADMASTER. We've all got to do things that go against the
grain, Golansky. That's what we try and teach you here.
Character-forming things. You know, I'm afraid you made
rather an exhibition of yourself.

DAVID. Yes. . . .

HEADMASTER. The other boys don't take that sort of thing to their hearts. Normally a boy wants to conform. To do as his classmates do. I mean . . . you wouldn't want to come to school in brown shoes, would you? Or in any sort of (*He laughs.*) cloth cap?

DAVID (*uncertain*). No. . . .

HEADMASTER. Of course, a boy in that type of attire would stick out . . . like a sore thumb! So try not to be an exception. Otherwise, I can promise, your life will be full of sorrow! The lot of a rebel, Golansky, is not to be envied!

DAVID. I suppose not.

HEADMASTER. And I don't want to see a boy unhappy.

DAVID. No, sir.

HEADMASTER. So, do something for me, will you?

DAVID. What?

HEADMASTER. Next Thursday, old man . . . (*He pleads.*) see if you can't hit him. Oh, nothing very violent. Just a little tap? Just to please me?

DAVID (*doubtful*). Well . . .

HEADMASTER. You'll find it a lot better than drawing attention to yourself!

DAVID (*miserable*). I suppose so. . . .

HEADMASTER. Good lad! So what do you say next Thursday . . . just land one on him. For me?

DAVID *looks miserable.*

All right. Cut along now . . . Go and get into a good healthy scrap somewhere! When "Chippy" and I aren't looking.

The HEADMASTER *winks nervously behind his glasses and attempts a hearty laugh.* DAVID *trails out.*

WIFE. Not our sort of boy.

HEADMASTER. I'm afraid you're right. The home influence creeping in again. Lives in an *hotel*, I believe!

WIFE. George!

HEADMASTER. Yes, dear.

WIFE. Hand me the wire, and remember, HOLD IT TIGHT!

5. The Resident's Lounge of the Hill-Top View Hotel: It is tea-time in this small private hotel. Old women are playing patience, old men are reading papers, as DAVID *walks past them.*

MINNIE *is getting the teas at the end of the room.* DAVID *takes a sandwich and starts to munch it. They talk in whispers.*

MINNIE. Your father's waiting to have tea with you.

DAVID. He'll have eaten all the sandwiches.

MINNIE. Don't say that, David. What's the matter, anyway? You look like a Sunday evening . . .

DAVID. Do you get . . . frightened, Minnie?

MINNIE. Frightened? Not just lately. Past it, perhaps.

DAVID. When you were young?

MINNIE. In the blitzes. Down the shelters we did. We used to sing.

DAVID. Sing?

MINNIE. That's the way. A sing-up! Lets the air in, where it's most required!

DAVID. I never thought of singing. . . .

MINNIE. Go on. Your father's eagerly awaiting you. . . .

At the end of the lounge MR. GOLANSKY *is having tea. He is eating a sandwich and the plate is almost empty. He is a spreading, balding, middle-aged man who varies between great cheerfulness and sudden despair, particularly in his relations with* DAVID. *He is almost too anxious to please, and he is often hurt and punctured by his lack of success when he brings himself to notice it. He shouts heartily as*

*DAVID comes up, and makes mock boxing gestures while
DAVID winces, sighs and sits down.*

MR. GOLANSKY. How's the old horse thief? . . . One to the
body, two to the body.

DAVID. I wish people would stop *doing* that!

The residents glare. MR. GOLANSKY *lowers his voice.*

MR. GOLANSKY. Enjoy your day?

DAVID. Not very much. . . .

MR. GOLANSKY (*pained*). Don't adopt that attitude, David. It's
a struggle for me to send you to that school.

A pause while DAVID *takes out his homework and begins on
it.*

You are happy there, aren't you, David? I only hope and
pray you're happy. If you weren't, if I ever thought you
weren't enjoying every living moment of it, I'd . . .

DAVID. What?

MR. GOLANSKY. I'd take you away, of course.

DAVID (*hopeful*). Before next Thursday?

MR. GOLANSKY (*in retreat*). Well, that's before the end of the
term and we *are* paid up . . . I mean, there's the business
to consider, and, say what you like, it does allow me to give
you the private fee-paying education which is an inestimable
advantage in this cut-throat community, David.

DAVID. I suppose so.

Pause.

MR. GOLANSKY. We understand each other, don't we, David?
I mean, we get on well, we keep each other company.

DAVID. Yes. (*He gets on with his homework.*)

MR. GOLANSKY. Well, we're thrown a lot together, stands to
reason. And I want to make it a pleasure for you . . . all
the time. What are those little objects? (*He looks at* DAVID'S
exercise book.)

DAVID. One-celled protoplasmic globules. . . .

MR. GOLANSKY. Go on! What are they doing then?

DAVID. Splitting in two.

MR. GOLANSKY. With what object, David?

DAVID. Renewing life.

MR. GOLANSKY. Renewing life? Well, there you are, you see! How strange you are, David.

DAVID. It's science.

MR. GOLANSKY. Yes, I suppose it is. Look, if there's something on your mind at any time . . . I'm the natural and proper person for you to confide in.

DAVID (*looks at him*). *He frightens me.*

MR. GOLANSKY (*pleased at the confidence*). Who? Who frightens you?

DAVID (*retreating*). Just . . . someone.

MR. GOLANSKY. I know how it feels, David. Of course I can understand. And I tell you what to do. Forget it! Put it out of your mind! We'll find something . . . A treat! Like tonight. We'll have dinner in here. Just the two of us. Your favourite. Roast chicken!

> *To* MINNIE *as she comes to clear away.*

Minnie. What's on tonight?

MINNIE. Fish!

MR. GOLANSKY (*deflated*). Oh! You don't like fish, do you? Well, on Saturday, then, we'll take the bird . . . There now, that cheers you up no end.

DAVID. I suppose so.

MR. GOLANSKY. Something to look forward to, and you can soon forget the unpleasant side. I've found that often, David. When something disagreeable looms up, just fix your thoughts on . . . Christmas.

DAVID (*gloomy*). It's January.

MR. GOLANSKY. Well, the long evenings to come! The days'll soon draw out and we'll run down to the coast. Fix your attention on that!

6. DAVID'S *bedroom: An ordinary hotel bedroom, bare and characterless. Moonlight is streaming in through the window.* DAVID *is asleep. His glider, which he will take to school in the morning, is on the dressing-table.*

We go in to a close-up of DAVID'S *face as he sleeps. Strange music introduces* DAVID'S *dream.*

7. DAVID'S *dream: Stars, planets, and comets are swimming in outer space.*

A rocket goes past in which are DAVID *and other boys in space helmets.* DAVID *is talking down the intercom.*

DAVID. Saucer to earth! Saucer to earth! Are you receiving me, earth? This is Captain Golansky. Are you receiving me? Am just about to make descent on Mars. Planet now visible, will lead landing party on arrival. THERE IS NO SIGN OF ANY LIVING CREATURE!

Shot of Mars approaching camera. The rocket lands. Swirling mist.
DAVID *is leading the other boys. The music is slow and rhythmical and gradually merges into the sound of heavy footsteps approaching through the mist.*

Keep together, men!

DAVID *is alone. He looks round desperately as the footsteps get louder.*

I think . . . there may be life here after all!

He looks up in terror. Slowly the immense face of BROCCOLI *appears through the mist. His great tentacled hands are stretched towards* DAVID. DAVID *screams.*

8. DAVID'S *bedroom:* MR. GOLANSKY *is sitting on* DAVID'S *bed and the light is on.* DAVID *is awake.*

MR. GOLANSKY. What is it, David old chap . . . what is it?

DAVID. *He was there!*

MR. GOLANSKY. It's late, old fellow . . .

DAVID. Wherever you go . . . *he's still there!*

MR. GOLANSKY. Who is, David? Who do you mean, old fellow?

DAVID. Him! You don't understand!

MR. GOLANSKY. There now, David . . . go to sleep. It'll look different by daylight. Things always look . . . better by the light of day.

> DAVID *turns his head away from him into the pillow.* MR. GOLANSKY *gestures at him hopelessly.*

9. The Assembly. Next morning: The HEADMASTER *is reading out prayers. As he does so, we see* DAVID *kneeling and peeping through his fingers and whispering to the* BOY *next to him. We also see the* HEADMASTER'S WIFE *as she frowns, and* DAVID'S *whispers are drowned by his loud and fervent amens. We also see* BROCCOLI *looking large and menacing behind the* HEAD-MASTER *on the platform.*

HEADMASTER (*continuing under the* BOYS' *dialogue*). Lighten our darkness we beseech thee, and by thy great mercy defend us from all perils of the night, for the love of thy only Son, our saviour Jesus Christ . . . Mercifully assist our prayers that we make before thee in all our troubles and adversities whensoever they oppress us; and graciously hear us that those evils which the craft and subtlety of the devil or man worketh against us may be brought to nought . . . Strengthen such as do stand, and comfort and help the weak-hearted; and finally beat down Satan under our feet.

DAVID. I've got a new glider.

BOY. Amen.

DAVID. In my locker. Gliders are my craze.

BOY. Who cares?

DAVID. I'll show it you after prayers—if you like. AMEN.

BOTH. AMEN.

They shuffle off their knees and the HEADMASTER *continues:*

HEADMASTER. Certain envelopes have been found behind the gymnasium apparently containing unwanted portions of school lunch. This disgusting and extravagant practice must stop immediately. The school visit will be paid next Thursday by the Bishop. The Bishop will be present at morning assembly and will visit the school activities including bouts of boxing under the supervision of the school professional. It is to be hoped that boys will not pull their punches and will give the Bishop a really good display of fighting. The Bishop, having been a well-known amateur middle-weight in his younger days, no doubt packs a good straight left if the occasion demands!

Obedient laughter, in which the HEADMASTER *joins.*

The School song will be sung next Thursday. We will now practise the first verse. . . .

The BOYS *stand and sing to the wheezing of the harmonium.*

BOYS. St. Alfred's boys, St. Alfred's boys
    Are scattered far and wide,
    St. Alfred's boys, St. Alfred's boys
    Have a deep warm glow inside . . .
    Whether in desert or in snow,
    They play the game of LIFE.
    They join in the hymn
    To their days in the gym . . .
    Where they learnt through
    Manly strife. . . .

10. The Changing-Room: DAVID *enters with the boy he was whispering to in prayers, and leads him to his locker. At the far*

end of the room BROCCOLI, *a king of the lockers, is holding forth
to his crowd of admiring boy subjects.*
DAVID (*opening the locker*). I made this one. . . .

> *The* BOY, *uninterested, has wandered off to listen to* BROC-
> COLI. DAVID *opens his locker and finds the glider gone.
> He looks up to where* BROCCOLI *is sitting and sees* BROC-
> COLI *is holding the glider.*

BROCCOLI. So there was this Brazilian, very heavy fighter, he
was, trained solely on raw meat and a solid granite punch
ball. That was the tale they told . . .

> DAVID *comes up to him.* BROCCOLI *has got* DAVID'S *glider
> in a great hand.*

All given out with a view to terrorizing the opposition. That
was the crafty side of it . . .
DAVID (*plucking up courage*). Excuse me. . . .
BROCCOLI (*taking no notice*). All right, I said, all right. Tell
him I train on sardines, and don't bother about taking them
out of the tins.
BOYS. You didn't say that! Oh, Broccoli! How *funny*. . . .
DAVID. Please, Mr. Smith.
BROCCOLI. Well, that was put out by my manager, Grumble
Johnson. He was a witty individual, believe you me.
DAVID. Could I have my glider now?
BROCCOLI. Marvellous-minded man. Never at a loss for the
witty word!
DAVID. Mr. Smith . . .
1ST BOY. Oh, shut up!
2ND BOY. He's telling us the story . . .
3RD BOY. Of the great fight.
DAVID. I just wanted . . .
1ST BOY (*pushes* DAVID *away*). *No thank you.*
BROCCOLI. So the bell went and I saw him blink. Always

blinked his eyes at a loud noise, and I thought, "Oi, oi. You can't see me . . . I can see you."

DAVID. I . . .

BROCCOLI (*to* DAVID). What've you come for? . . . To 'it me or something? . . .

1ST BOY (*laughing*). *No thank you!*

BROCCOLI (*comic cower*). Don't bash me too 'ard. I'm only a nipper!

BROCCOLI *and the* BOYS *roar with laughter.*

DAVID (*very quiet*). That glider . . .

BROCCOLI (*angry*). Regulations provide. No toys to be kept in lockers. Sports equipment only. Dispose of it!

BROCCOLI *hands over the glider, which is broken.*

DAVID. It's broken!

BROCCOLI *turns away from him and goes on with his story.*

BROCCOLI. And I remembered the instructions what Grumble gave me, which was to use my brains and box clever. And when I knew his world was dark, I crept up on him and . . .

DAVID. You broke it!

BROCCOLI. . . . whispered, "Come on, 'it me." Tantalizing him, you see, that's what I was doing . . . Tantalizing him crafty. Boxing clever. . . .

The BOY DAVID *brought to see the glider stays to listen to* BROCCOLI. DAVID *walks away alone, the broken glider in his hands.*

11. The School Boiler-Room: This small, warm shed is where DAVID *comes as a refuge to see his friend, the old gnome-like man who looks after the boiler and does odd jobs about the school.*

BOILERMAN. I'll give it a touch of glue when I've got a moment.

DAVID. He did it on purpose.

BOILERMAN. Broccoli? (*He puts the glider on a shelf.*) Scares you, doesn't he?

DAVID *nods.*

When's the next lesson?

DAVID. Thursday . . . I wish there wasn't a next Thursday.

BOILERMAN. Then it's . . . over the top? Like in the nineteen-fourteen. Over the top tomorrow, they said . . . and I thought, tomorrow is a day that wouldn't ever be missed. Let's go to sleep and wake up next summer. Of course they offered you comforts, tots of rum, nice hymn, new pair of khaki mittens knitted by her old ladyship in some nice, safe dugout in Wimbledon. There was I, like you, boy, staring straight in the face of danger. . . .

DAVID. What did you do?

BOILERMAN. Well, you had three alternatives. Go through with it, shoot yourself in the foot, or run away. Personally, I took my courage in both hands, and I runned away.

DAVID. That was brave. . . .

BOILERMAN. Damned stupid. I runned in the wrong direction. Slap into the Jerry trenches. Saw a young chap there and I said, "For God's sake give me a whiff of gas, just to put me under for the duration." Of course, not being educated, he couldn't understand what I was saying. He shot me in the hand, just lovely. They put me on cookhouse duties after that. They got some terrible meals. There was one Christmas dinner . . . Not fit for human consumption. We gave it to the officers. . . .

DAVID. Does it hurt much? Being shot in the hand?

BOILERMAN. No . . . irritates a bit, that's all. Here. Don't you go and get ideas, now. Don't you go to the length of self-inflicted wounds . . . He's not so bad, old Broccoli. Well, just a bit horrible, perhaps. He can't help that. It's his living. He comes in here, with those magazines what he reads . . . and talks about the end of the world. . . .

DAVID. The what?

BOILERMAN. He's got it fixed for the year three thousand. Says it's a mathematical certainty. Well, it's got to end some time, hasn't it? I mean, it just can't go on and on, stands to reason.

DAVID. No.

BOILERMAN. But he gives us till the year three thousand. . . .

DAVID. That's a long time. . . .

BOILERMAN. It'll see him out, anyway.

DAVID. I wish it was next Thursday!

BOILERMAN. What?

DAVID. The end of the world.

BOILERMAN. Why . . . Oh, I see. To stop the lesson.

DAVID *nods*.

You'd carry it to those lengths?

DAVID. If I could put a stop to it. . . .

BOILERMAN. You've got a very brilliant brain, I don't doubt.

DAVID. Quite clever. . . .

BOILERMAN. Which is where you'll finally be one up on Mr. Smith.

DAVID (*incredulous*). I will?

BOILERMAN. I don't doubt that, boy. But leave the rest of the Universe alone, will you? Do me a great favour. Leave the world turning until next Saturday week. I haven't got my peas planted, not yet. . . .

12. The Classroom: The lesson is just finishing. DAVID *is listening attentively as the* HEADMASTER *chalks on the blackboard and explains.*

HEADMASTER (*in one breath*). Julius Caesar's Calendar was misunderstood by priests and supposes the year to be too long by approximately 11 minutes, 14 seconds. The geocentric motion of the sun in longitude from the mean

Julian equinox up to date is 365·25 days, therefore 360 degrees plus 27·685 gives us the length of the solar year in the formula

$$\frac{360}{360 \times 27 \cdot 685} = 365 \cdot 25 = 365 \cdot 2422.$$

This led to the equinox slowly moving backwards, and by the year 1582 three days had disappeared in every four hundred years. This was corrected by ten days being suppressed in the calendar. . . .

The bell rings.

Does everyone understand?
BOYS (*as they rush out*). Oh yes, sir! Perfectly, sir!

DAVID *walks slowly past the blackboard. He looks at the figures.*

HEADMASTER. You understand, Golansky?

DAVID *looks carefully in silence at the figures.*

13. *The School Playground: The* BOYS *are all playing and milling about. A group are boasting to each other.*

1ST BOY. We've got an electric pancake mixer!
2ND BOY. We've got a darning machine that lights up!
4TH BOY. We've got a lovely thing over the sink that squirts hand cream out of it. . . .
DAVID. We've got a potato peeler for seventy people. . . .
3RD BOY. Liar! Where?
DAVID. In the hotel. Minnie uses it.
3RD BOY. It isn't yours, then.
1ST BOY. Not yours, "No thank you."
2ND BOY. Who wants to live in a stinky hotel?
3RD BOY. My mother can't *bear* hotel life. She told my father that.

DAVID *wanders away from them. He kicks a stone. He gives it a great kick and it skitters across the playground and stops by an enormous foot. The foot is* BROCCOLI'S. DAVID *starts to back away.* BROCCOLI *is standing by a wall in a distant part of the playground. He has a bit of chalk and the wall is covered with figures. He lifts his hand at* DAVID.

BROCCOLI. Get out. . . .

DAVID. I'm sorry, Mr. Smith. . . .

BROCCOLI. What's that?

DAVID. I'm sorry, sir.

BROCCOLI *advances,* DAVID *retreats against the wall.*

BROCCOLI. Playground not big enough . . . Not enough space available for your recreation?

DAVID. No, it's not that, I . . .

BROCCOLI. Or did they (*He points to the figures on the wall.*) attract your curiosity?

DAVID. I didn't notice them. . . .

BROCCOLI. No!

DAVID. Honestly!

BROCCOLI. But you sees them now, don't you?

DAVID. Yes.

BROCCOLI (*proud*). And they *bewilders* you, don't they. (*He mimics* DAVID.) Honestly?

DAVID. Just a bit, sir.

BROCCOLI. I thought they'd baffle you. Come on, use your education on that lot!

DAVID. Looks like a great big . . . multiply.

BROCCOLI. Big? You may call it big. It's nothing less than . . . the future of mankind!

DAVID. That's very interesting.

BROCCOLI. I dare say it is interesting. You study this at school?

He takes a tattered book from his pocket.

L.H.–G

Everyman's Almanac and chart of future events. Based on
the solar equinox! Do they learn you any of that?

DAVID. Not . . . quite, Mr. Broccoli.

BROCCOLI. Ah. About time they did then, isn't it?

DAVID. There's lots they . . . don't tell us.

BROCCOLI. Gaps in your education?

DAVID. Oh, yes . . . great big gaps.

BROCCOLI. I mean, they give you the past, don't they? They
give you plenty of that!

DAVID. Quite a lot.

BROCCOLI. Then why don't they give you the future? Out of
this where it's been carefully charted out! Why don't they
give you that?

DAVID. I wish they would . . . in some period or other.

BROCCOLI. I bet you do. Useful knowledge, this . . . very
useful knowledge. Now, if you're backward at all . . . no
doubt it would be to your advantage to have some of this
imparted to you.

DAVID. No doubt at all, Mr. Broccoli.

DAVID *is backing away.* BROCCOLI *grabs his wrist.*

BROCCOLI. Come here, boy. What you got? A nervous disposition?

DAVID. Just a bit.

BROCCOLI. Well, that's no good to you. Where do you think
I'd have got with a nervous disposition?

DAVID. Nowhere, I suppose.

BROCCOLI. Not to be the household word of the West Ham
Stadium! Not to get those cheers thrown at you like money!
A few laughs . . . that's all you'd win from a nervous
disposition.

DAVID. I suppose so.

BROCCOLI. Draw up then. . . .

DAVID *does so, nervously.*

You see, there it is, all set out in date order! Taken straight
from the almanac of forecasts . . . Dating from the first
rising of the sun and having due regard to the orbit of the
moon. Every date you could wish to see mentioned. The
Armada, Mafeking . . . The loss of the *Titanic* too . . .
Chelsea's Cup Final . . . Armageddon . . . and . . .
THE END.

DAVID. The end?

BROCCOLI. Of the world!

Pause. DAVID *takes a great breath.*

DAVID. Well, it can't last for ever . . . Oh, they taught us
about that!

BROCCOLI. They did?

DAVID. Oh, yes.

BROCCOLI. I'm glad they taught you *something*.

DAVID. In Ancient History. To start with, the world came
spinning off the sun red hot, just like a red-hot cricket ball.
And then there were these one-celled protoplasmic objects
in these swamps and things. Renewing life. Well, they can't
keep it up for ever . . . And all that spinning, it's got to
slow down some time. It stands to reason. I mean, there are
already signs. Cracks and things! And the stars . . . *they're
not as bright as they used to be!*

BROCCOLI. What are you saying?

DAVID (*sepulchral*). We're approaching the end, Mr. Smith.

BROCCOLI. Did they tell you . . . what it's going to be like?

DAVID. Well . . . not really. Not exactly, that is. But cold, I
should imagine, and sort of . . . grey. And nothing there.
No life I mean. (*Eagerly.*) No life at all!

BROCCOLI. 'Orrible!

He is impressed. DAVID *looks at him curiously.*

DAVID. Or perhaps just . . . complete disintegration. . . .

BROCCOLI. How 'orrible! (*He puts his hand across his eyes.*)

DAVID. And the worst of it is . . . it might happen so soon!

BROCCOLI. Soon?

DAVID. Yes. . . .

BROCCOLI. By when?

DAVID. Next Thursday . . . before the lesson . . . (*His confidence drains away*.) It might be by next Thursday. . . .

    BROCCOLI *looks up, his face smiling.*

BROCCOLI (*laughs*). No! There's more than a thousand years . . . before the great day! We've got all that time. To go on 'itting each other.

    Pause.

DAVID. You're *sure*?

BROCCOLI. Them figures. They proves it. Figures worked out, by them that had education.

DAVID (*looking at the figures*). Whoever worked out the last line forgot to carry the fourteen.

BROCCOLI (*frowns*). They did?

DAVID. Of course, it may not be important.

BROCCOLI (*doubtful*). That your strong suit? The mathematics?

DAVID (*quietly*). I got an honour mark, in sums.

BROCCOLI (*impressed*). You did?

DAVID. Last term I got an honourable mention, and this term I'll get the prize.

BROCCOLI. Then you can see how it's worked out. It gives us a bit of breathing space.

DAVID. I'm not . . . sure.

BROCCOLI. How do you mean? Not sure. (*He looks at* DAVID *with deep suspicion*.) Not trying to . . . frighten me, by any stretch of the imagination?

DAVID. Oh, no, sir! All the same, I'm afraid . . .

BROCCOLI. What of?

DAVID. Your maths. It may not be your best subject!

BROCCOLI. No. . . .

DAVID (*helpful*). Look here, Mr. Smith. Would you like me to check those figures over for you? I could do it tonight at home. With my instruments.

BROCCOLI. What?

DAVID. Slide rule.

BROCCOLI. Oh. . . .

DAVID. We'd be quite sure then, wouldn't we?

BROCCOLI. We would?

DAVID. Oh, yes. It's very safe. Of course, I won't unless you'd like me to. . . .

BROCCOLI. Would it be much trouble . . . for you, I mean?

DAVID (*looking critically at the figures*). Oh, I shouldn't think so . . . I'll just run the slide rule over them. It might . . . set your mind at rest.

BROCCOLI. If you have the opportunity. . . .

DAVID. Leave it to me, sir. (*He takes the paper.*)

BROCCOLI. At a convenient moment! Honourable mention!

DAVID. Oh, it . . . was nothing really. I'll tell you the result tomorrow.

BROCCOLI. I can't seem to settle to anything. Not till I know for certain . . . how long we've got.

He frowns at DAVID *and shuffles doubtfully off.* DAVID *watches him go.*

14. The Hotel Lounge. Late in the afternoon: MR. GOLANSKY *is having his tea.* MINNIE *passes him and looks up at the clock.*

MINNIE. David's late. . . .

MR. GOLANSKY. Up to some . . . scrape or other.

MINNIE. Scrape?

MR. GOLANSKY. You know what boys are, Minnie. Torn trousers, black eyes. Late home from school because they've got involved in some type of rough and tumble!

MINNIE. I always thought David was the quiet type. . . .

MR. GOLANSKY. *Quiet*, Minnie?

MINNIE. Serious.

MR. GOLANSKY. He's not serious. Takes after me!

MINNIE. Well, you're lighthearted, Mr. Golansky, as we know.

MR. GOLANSKY. You've got to be. With things as they are.

MINNIE (*sympathetic*). Of course, you have your worries. Kids don't understand that, do they?

MR. GOLANSKY. You're right, they don't realize. No business worries for *them*! No bills! No communications from the Commissioners of Inland Revenue! (*He takes a tablet.*) No indigestion!

MINNIE. Still, he looks serious to me, David.

MR. GOLANSKY (*laughs*). Not him. Why, if he had anything to be serious about do you think I wouldn't know it? Telepathic, that's what we two've been. Since I lost his mother that is.

MINNIE. You lost her?

MR. GOLANSKY. That's about the right word!

MINNIE. Of course, we know nothing, Mr. Golansky, in the Hill-Top View. Except the way you look after David. Not that I've ever had offspring myself. . . .

MR. GOLANSKY. We were living in the country at the time— Mrs. Golansky and self. You won't believe this, but I had some people to meet, business acquaintances, and we got in the local licensed premises. Anyway, I said I'd meet her under the market clock. Well, you know how it is with business acquaintances. It got a bit over the hour . . . and when I went to look for her, she was gone! She'd posted herself as missing! And I'd got something laid on, in the enjoyment line, for that very evening!

MINNIE. She left you with David?

MR. GOLANSKY. She'd often threatened to leave me with the responsibility. So anyway, the home was broken up, we moved to town to be nearer the business, and since then it's been hotel accommodation! If she'd only have waited half an hour she'd have found I had something arranged . . . Although her chief pleasure seemed to lie in the opening of unpleasant communications.

MINNIE. Communications. . . .

MR. GOLANSKY. Oh, we had our difficult times. And bills were dropping through the door, brown and threatening. Well, file those away, I'd say, and let's plan something pleasant. . . .

MINNIE. Very understandable.

MR. GOLANSKY. If you continually open bills no wonder you take to flight!

MINNIE. Here he comes . . .

DAVID *crosses the lounge towards them.*

Now don't you see it? The serious look.

MR. GOLANSKY (*laughs*). That young man's got nothing more serious on his mind than the treat of tomorrow's dinner.

MINNIE. You'll both be taking the bird?

MR. GOLANSKY. You bet we will! (*To* DAVID.) How's the old horse-thief?

DAVID *sits down and undoes his satchel. He takes out a paper-covered book and a slide rule and begins calculations.*

MINNIE. He studies hard.

MR. GOLANSKY (*excusing* DAVID). The minimum he has to! Homework, eh, David?

DAVID. No. It's actually something I'm . . . working out for myself.

MR. GOLANSKY (*taken aback*). Private study? Well, I like to see a boy carry out a programme of private study. What's it for, David?

DAVID. Just to settle a question that's arisen. . . .

MR. GOLANSKY. Arisen? Who with, David?

DAVID. Just someone I know. (*Working.*) I want to see which of us is right.

MR. GOLANSKY. Sporting, you see! I bet there's a few marbles staked on this one! (DAVID *winces.*) What do you get if you win, David?

DAVID. Oh, I don't get anything. But if he's wrong . . .

MINNIE. What, David?

DAVID (*quietly*). He'll be *obliterated*!

15. BROCCOLI'S *Room. Next day: A bare and miserable room with the bed unmade.* BROCCOLI *is at the window giving birdseed to a small canary in a large and homemade cage. There is a small knock at the door which* BROCCOLI *does not hear.*

The door is pushed open. DAVID *is standing timidly close to the door.* BROCCOLI *turns and roars.*

BROCCOLI. Get out!

> DAVID *shrinks against the wall but does not go.* BROCCOLI *blinks as he turns from the window.*

This is my private quarters . . . Who let you up here?

DAVID. I just came to say . . .

BROCCOLI (*blinks*). It's you again. . . .

DAVID. I checked those figures for you.

BROCCOLI (*shouts*). NO BOYS ALLOWED!

DAVID. You seemed so anxious about the figures, I thought you wouldn't mind if I came.

BROCCOLI. Well, I do mind. An interruption. In my quarters!

DAVID. I'm sorry, sir. (*Pause. He holds out a bit of paper.*) I've got the answer to your problem, sir. It's quite reliable. . . .

BROCCOLI. What?

DAVID. I checked them with the use of decimals. I'm afraid there can't be a mistake!

BROCCOLI. With the use of decimals! That'll be part of your private education?

DAVID. Oh yes, Mr. Smith.

BROCCOLI. Old Grumble Johnson used to tell me, you don't need no private education. No fighting boy needs to be able to count above ten . . . eight, nine, ten, he used to say . . . and after that, you lose interest! A very witty individual.

DAVID. He must have been *killing*!

BROCCOLI. Well, you've worked it out. Bright at your lessons, I take it?

DAVID. At maths I am. I'm awfully weak on nature.

BROCCOLI. Nature!

DAVID. It's all about . . . pollen.

BROCCOLI. Yes . . . when I was a nipper we had a Miss come down to our school . . . She was connected with charity. "You boys," she said, "is weak on nature." So she took us out on a train, somewhere in the direction of Ruislip which was then a rural community. And I remember, clear as you stand there, saying, "God, Miss, what's those awful animals?" And she said, "Ain't you seen one before? Cows." I was scared.

DAVID. You were frightened?

BROCCOLI. The first and last time, I assure you.

DAVID. Good.

BROCCOLI. Why?

DAVID. I've got some disturbing news . . . You may find it a bit disappointing. . . .

BROCCOLI. What.

DAVID. Those figures . . .

BROCCOLI. Yes?

DAVID. . . . are not strictly accurate. . . .

BROCCOLI. They've never been doubted!

DAVID. It's the fault of the calendar. There was that Julius Caesar. He got years wrong in the first place. And his priests were pretty dim about the whole thing, if you ask me. Anyway, he made the years too long by about . . . oh, months really. And that time-table of yours . . . hasn't recognized the fact!

BROCCOLI (*gulps*). Does that make any difference?

DAVID. Oh, yes. Quite a bit, mathematically, that is . . . It mightn't have been so bad if they hadn't tried to put it right later.

BROCCOLI. Put it right?

DAVID. In 1582 they suppressed another ten days. You see, the calendar doesn't bear much relation . . . to the passage of time.

BROCCOLI. It's gone by without us knowing it?

DAVID. That's right. You see, all those mistakes have shortened the time quite considerably, so . . .

BROCCOLI. What?

DAVID. Well, I've worked it out and it comes to . . . starting at the first mean equinox, about . . . two and a half days left!

BROCCOLI. You mean . . . ?

DAVID. What is it now . . . Monday. That gives us . . . until some time on Wednesday night. Probably after midnight.

BROCCOLI. And then . . . ?

DAVID. I don't suppose there'll be a lesson on Thursday.

BROCCOLI (*whispers*). What . . . will there be?

DAVID. A storm. I should think it'll begin with a storm. Lightning and that sort of thing.

BROCCOLI. And then?

> DAVID *shrugs his shoulders. Pause.*

You're having your . . . little joke.

DAVID. I wish I was. It's the figures, you see, Mr. Smith. They just work out that way. . . .

BROCCOLI. I don't understand . . .

DAVID (*sympathetic*). No . . .

BROCCOLI. You've made a mistake!

DAVID. I wish I had, honestly I do. But I kept on checking it. It came out as Thursday every time!

BROCCOLI. Thursday!

DAVID. Don't worry, Mr. Smith. It probably won't hurt—
BROCCOLI. The finish! (*He rubs his head.*)
DAVID. You shouldn't worry. After all, it'd come as a surprise, if you hadn't got so interested in the arithmetic!

> BROCCOLI *tears his almanac across with a sudden gesture of his huge hands.*

I mean . . . it's got to end some time, as I told you. It would be just as awful, if it went on for ever. It's got to end. It's only . . . we've been selected to be here when it does.
BROCCOLI (*staring vacantly in front of him*). Selected!
DAVID. A sort of honour really. The last men in the world!

> DAVID *tiptoes out.* BROCCOLI *shudders. His head sinks into his great hands.*

16. The Assembly. Next day: The HEADMASTER *is addressing the Assembly. During the reading a calm and contemptuous* DAVID *is looking at a desperate and shivering* BROCCOLI *sitting behind the* HEADMASTER.

HEADMASTER. Today's lesson is from 1 Samuel, chapter 17, verse 46: "This day will the Lord deliver thee into mine hand; and I will smite thee, and take thine head from off thee; and I will give the carcasses of the host of the Philistines this day unto the fowls of the air, and to the wild beasts of the earth; that all the earth may know that there is a God in Israel; and that this assembly may know that the Lord saveth not with a sword and a spear; for the battle is the Lord's and he will give you into our hand. So David prevailed over the Philistine with a sling and a stone, and smote the Philistine and slew him. But there was no sword in the hand of David."
Before prayers I will remind the school that today, instead of the usual Wednesday games period, there will be an extra rehearsal of the school song in readiness for tomorrow's visit

from the Bishop. A really rousing rendering of our lovely song, which as you know is the work of an old boy, the present editor of the *North Boscombe Sentinel*, C. P. K. Waller, is compulsory on this occasion.

17. The Boiler Room: The BOILERMAN *is eating his sand-wiches.* BROCCOLI *is hunched in the doorway looking up at the sky.*

BROCCOLI. It isn't raining. . . .

BOILERMAN. You said that before.

BROCCOLI. There's no clouds.

BOILERMAN. Go on. Cheer up. Have a sandwich?

> *He goes to* BROCCOLI, *offering his paper of sandwiches.* BROCCOLI *pushes them away.*

All right. I only offered. A bit of tea?

BROCCOLI. I don't want no tea.

BOILERMAN. It's good meat. Comes from the market, down our way. It's good. The meat from our market. (*He chews.*) Nice and fresh. What's the matter with you? Don't you fancy no sandwiches?

BROCCOLI. There's a cloud. Up there.

BOILERMAN. Not dainty enough for you?

BROCCOLI. It'll blow away. It's travelling fast.

BOILERMAN. What is?

BROCCOLI. That cloud.

BOILERMAN. I don't know what you're talking about half the time.

BROCCOLI. Ah. . . .

BOILERMAN. What you mean . . . ah?

BROCCOLI. Better you don't know.

BOILERMAN. What?

BROCCOLI. I said, better you keep ignorant.

BOILERMAN. Ignorant. Well, I like that! The day you start, Mr. Smith, referring to the ignorance of others.

BROCCOLI. It's growing.

BOILERMAN. What?

BROCCOLI. That cloud I mentioned.

BOILERMAN. Cheer up. Gives a person a revolting feeling, listening to you on about the state of the weather. Come on. (*He reads the paper round his sandwiches.*) Here's something that'll interest you. "The stars foretell . . ."

BROCCOLI. Can't you keep quiet!

BOILERMAN. "Taurus the Bull." That's you, ain't it? "Taurus the Bull. A good day for putting your affairs in order." What the . . .

> BROCCOLI *has hit the paper with his fist and torn it. The* BOILERMAN *looks at him bewildered as* BROCCOLI *goes. As he shambles off he sees* DAVID *crossing to the boiler-room.* BROCCOLI'S *head sinks. He goes off, avoiding* DAVID'S *eye.*

DAVID (*brightly*). It's clouding over.

BOILERMAN. Not you, too!

DAVID. It's going to get . . . lovely and black!

BOILERMAN. Oh . . . have a sandwich.

DAVID. All right. (*He eats.*) They're delicious.

BOILERMAN. Good market down our way. (*Pause.*) What's the matter with him?

DAVID. Who?

BOILERMAN. Broccoli Smith. West Ham's world-famed Paper Doll.

DAVID. Paper what?

BOILERMAN. Not part of your vocabulary. . . .

DAVID (*lying*). Oh, yes, I know what that means.

BOILERMAN. Then you should sympathize.

DAVID. *I* should?

BOILERMAN. I mean, he was never exactly one for sprightly repartee, as we know. But now he's dead silent. Even seems to have lost interest in the future!

DAVID (*casually*). Has he?

BOILERMAN. Never speaks of it. Seems remote from him somehow . . . Comes in here . . . just for a warm, and stands . . . "Cheer up," I tell him. "We're not dead yet."

DAVID. Does it cheer him up, when you say that to him?

BOILERMAN. Not particularly, now I come to think of it . . . And you seem different somehow. . . .

DAVID. Me?

BOILERMAN. As I look at you. You was always, on the solemn side. And now, you seem . . . exalted!

DAVID. What?

BOILERMAN. In the nineteen fourteen we had them. They'd come out young and serious, and the fighting made them . . . excited. They was always laughing and joking. Made you uneasy to listen to them. Yes . . . you seems more lively to me now, as if you'd had a bit of secret leave in Paris. . . .

DAVID. I swear I haven't!

BOILERMAN. Of course not. No leave for you, is there?

DAVID. Look . . . (*He is looking out of the door.*)

BOILERMAN. What?

DAVID. It's raining. . . .

BOILERMAN. Well?

DAVID. There's going to be a storm. (*Excited.*) It's Wednesday night . . . and there's going to be a storm.

> DAVID *runs away across the wet playground, through the rain, splashing in the puddles.* BROCCOLI *is standing in a doorway sheltering. He looks up in horror at the thunder and lightning in the sky. The water pours down his beaten-up and frightened face.*
>
> DAVID *calls out to him as he runs by, and doesn't wait for an answer.*

DAVID. Good night, Mr. Smith. (*And fainter as he runs.*) Goodbye, Mr. Smith. . . .

18. BROCCOLI'S *Room. That night:* BROCCOLI *in his pyjamas is standing at the open window of his room and looking up at the storm. He opens the door of the birdcage and releases the bird. It flies away into the stormy darkness.*

19. The Playground. Next morning: It is very quiet and still. The sun is rapidly drying up the puddles on the playground. The school bell finishes ringing.

20. The Assembly. Next morning: The HEADMASTER *is on the platform, conducting the singing of the school song. The* BOYS *are singing.* DAVID *is looking at* BROCCOLI'S *empty place. The* BISHOP, *looking remarkably pugilistic, grins. The* HEAD-MASTER'S WIFE *is bent over the harmonium.*

21. BROCCOLI'S *Bedroom:* BROCCOLI *is in bed, the clothes over his head. The sound of* BOYS *singing as a distant and angelic choir gently filters into the room. He slowly emerges from the bedclothes and blinks in the sunlight. He puts up his hand and gently, uncertainly, pulls his ear. He gradually gets out of bed and puts his foot to the floor. His toes grope. To his obvious surprise they find solid floor.*

22. The Assembly: Back to the school singing. A dignified occasion.

23. BROCCOLI'S *Bedroom:* BROCCOLI *is exploring the room in his pyjamas, touching and feeling familiar objects. He blinks in the sun.*

24. The Staircase: BROCCOLI *has emerged from his room and is descending the staircase. He is like a sleep-walker, but as his hand caresses the solid banister he begins to smile.*

25. The Assembly: The school is still singing.

Suddenly we see the BISHOP'S *face as the song dies in amazement on his lips.*

The HEADMASTER *is silent and amazed.*

The singing dies all round.

BROCCOLI *has thrown open the Hall door and is standing in his pyjamas, his arms thrown out wide as he roars in triumph:*

BROCCOLI. We're still here. Look at us! We're alive!

> DAVID'S *face is impassive and inscrutable behind his glasses in his moment of triumph.*

26. *The Playground: The crowd of* BOYS *are puzzled, whispering together, unable to understand what has happened.* DAVID *comes striding among them.*

In the following scene, DAVID'S *excitement and elation, which is on the edge of hysteria, infects the other* BOYS, *so that the moody and doubtful silence in which this scene begins ends with a deafening excitement.*

DAVID (*throwing up his arms*). We're alive! Latest news, and stale buns, we're all very much alive! Tell the Bishop, tell the Headmaster! We're living and breathing. . . .

1ST BOY. We *know.*

2ND BOY. Why did he tell us *that*?

3RD BOY. With his pyjamas on?

DAVID. You want to know? Give you three guesses? Animal, vegetable or mineral. . . .

BOYS. Tell us. . . .

DAVID. You're getting warm, you're getting cold.

BOYS. We don't know.

DAVID. Give you a clue?

1ST BOY. Yes.

DAVID. Where was Moses when the light went out?

2ND BOY. Stop it and tell!

1ST BOY. Why?

DAVID. Why does a bear wear a fur coat?

BOYS. WHY?

DAVID. It'd look silly in a mack!

1ST BOY. Stop it and tell us. . . .

4TH BOY. Please, David.

DAVID. See this wet, see this dry.

1ST BOY. It was funny. . . .

DAVID. Keep it dark till the day you die.

BOYS. Oh, stop it.

DAVID. I'll give you this very confidential information.

3RD BOY. Who do you think you are? . . .

DAVID. Dutch Martin . . . Battling Butcher! David Golan-sky! I . . . knocked . . . him out!

BOYS. Who?

DAVID. Broccoli! He's scared.

BOYS. What of?

DAVID. Me!

3RD BOY. You flea!

BOYS. Why? . . .

DAVID. I told . . . Listen, I said . . . I *proved it* to him.

BOYS. What?

DAVID. *Quod erat demonstrandum!* I said, "Poor old Broccoli, say your prayers. Prepare to meet your God. Thursday morning's going to be The Ending of the World!"

BOYS. He believed you?

DAVID. Hook, line and stinker!

BOYS. He thought it would?

DAVID. He genuinely did! And he woke up and found himself all in one bit. Poor old Broccoli was *glad*!

1ST BOY. He *must* have been scared!

2ND BOY. In a funk.

3RD BOY. Dead with fright.

DAVID. The world's ended!

1ST BOY. Then we're all dead.

2ND BOY. I'm dead!

1ST BOY. And you're dead!

L.H.–H

3RD BOY. I'm a ghost . . . (*Putting his mackintosh over his head.*) Whoooooooooo!

1ST BOY (*doing the same*). Eeeeeeeeee!

2ND BOY (*doing the same*). I'm a spooooooooook!

1ST BOY. Let's go and tell Broccoli!

3RD BOY. We're dead as doornails.

1ST BOY. Let's give him another scare. . . .

2ND BOY. Put the wind up Broccoli. . . .

3RD BOY. Whoooooo!

1ST BOY. Come on, David. . . .

2ND BOY. Get your mack, David. We'll be four great, dirty ghosts!

DAVID. I'll catch you up.

27. *The Boiler Room:* DAVID *runs in and gets his mack which has been hanging on a chair in front of the boiler to dry.*

BOILERMAN. Broccoli Smith's just been in.

DAVID (*casual*). Has he?

BOILERMAN. Interested?

DAVID. Not awfully.

BOILERMAN. He came to say goodbye.

DAVID. He's going?

BOILERMAN. Why don't you give a party?

DAVID. I didn't know. . . .

BOILERMAN. He tendered his reluctant resignation.

DAVID. Why does he have to . . . go?

BOILERMAN. You don't know?

DAVID. No, honestly.

BOILERMAN. Because if I was to appear in my night attire and inform the Bishop that there was still life in him, contrary to all appearances, I should also expect my cards. It appears someone of superior brain-power misled Mr. Smith about the date.

DAVID *is silent.*

You had the advantage over him.

DAVID. Me?

BOILERMAN. Stands to reason. You're young and he's got one foot in the New End Hospital. You can think clever and he has a job to remember what those long elastic loops buttoned on to his trousers are *for* every morning. You can laugh at him and he can't laugh at you. . . .

DAVID. He can't?

BOILERMAN. He takes it all serious. Which is what lays him open to attack.

DAVID. Attack?

BOILERMAN. A shot in the back. . . .

DAVID. I wouldn't . . .

BOILERMAN. You say that! But in the nineteen fourteen there was a sergeant. A bastard, of no mean variety. And a close friend of mine was determined to rid us of the presence of this complete blot. So he shot him during one of the fool-hardy attacks what we made. And after that he missed that bastard like hell in the mornings. He was his enemy—and he missed him like a friend!

Pause.

DAVID. He'll be all right, won't he?

BOILERMAN. What makes you think that?

DAVID. He's a champion.

BOILERMAN. I told you. He's a paper doll.

DAVID. I don't know what that means.

BOILERMAN. Oh, what do they insert into your head by way of education! Such a brilliant boxer! The only man he ever knocked out was the referee by a complete error of judgement. . . .

DAVID. No!

BOILERMAN. You owe a special duty of care . . . to that type of individual!

Pause.

BOY (*calling from outside*). Come on, David . . . You're being *hours*!

DAVID *hesitates, looks at the* BOILERMAN, *but finally goes.*

DAVID. All right . . . coming.

28. BROCCOLI'S *Room: The door is open and we hear the hoots, whooooos, and "we're spooks" of the* BOYS. BROCCOLI *roars. Three* BOYS *come running out and away down the passage.*

DAVID'S *mack has fallen to the ground and he is standing looking at the paper parcels and empty birdcage which is* BROCCOLI'S *luggage.*

BROCCOLI, *all rage spent, is exhausted and blinking.*

DAVID. It's gone.

BROCCOLI. What?

DAVID. Your bird.

BROCCOLI. Well, I'm going. I doubt if I'll have the accommodation.

DAVID. I see. . . .

BROCCOLI. It wasn't much of a canary. But leastways not a gaol bird. I made sure of that. . . .

DAVID. A what?

BROCCOLI. Blackbird or starling. Dyed yellow. Blokes'd do that, and flog 'em down the Lane. Gaol birds, we termed them . . . At least mine was the genuine article. It didn't sing much, though. Sex was all wrong, most likely. (*Pause.*) I was just going. You nearly missed me, with the reception committee. . . .

DAVID. I know. I'm sorry. . . .

BROCCOLI. What was that?

DAVID. I said, I'm sorry you have to go. I didn't mean . . .

BROCCOLI. You'll miss the lessons, eh? A lark to you lot, weren't they, them lessons?

DAVID (*weakly*). In a sort of way. . . .

BROCCOLI. It was a lark all right for you! 'Itting the instructor. Just a childish pastime. Not your careers.

DAVID. No, Mr. Smith, and I ought to tell you . . .

BROCCOLI. It might have been humiliation to me, what was enjoyment to you. Did you think of that?

DAVID. No. . . .

BROCCOLI. I got to dread those Thursdays. . . .

DAVID (amazed). You did?

BROCCOLI. The humiliation. I'm glad it's finished with.

DAVID. I didn't enjoy it, Mr. Smith.

BROCCOLI. Well, thank you for that.

Pause.

DAVID. That's all right.

Pause.

BROCCOLI. Now I can continue my career.

DAVID. Your career, Mr. Smith?

BROCCOLI. What do you think they'd say if they was to see me sitting here and being struck at by a load of thin-armed short-sighted nippers.

DAVID. They, Mr. Smith?

BROCCOLI. Sport Hughes. Pipe Logan. Grumble Johnson. Can you imagine?

DAVID. No, Mr. Smith.

BROCCOLI. They were good to me, them three. Not like some of the boys was treated. Regular meals. Dry bedding and ten per cent of your own prize money in your own pocket. But the game's changed. "You've got to box clever," Grumble told me. "You've got to box a bit clever against these Welsh boys. Smart, them Welsh monkeys." He was all right, old Grumble.

DAVID. He must have been.

BROCCOLI. So . . . I'm off anyway.

DAVID. If I could explain . . .

BROCCOLI. You never know when a bit of good luck is due to arrive. Like that very first day . . . I was discovered.

DAVID. You were lucky?

BROCCOLI. I was lucky all right. It was the outset of my career you see. I was walking slowly along. Somewhere in the Islington area. With a young lady . . . You wouldn't understand that.

DAVID. No. . . .

BROCCOLI. And all of a sudden some young chap called out at this young lady who was then holding my arm. (*Pause.*)

DAVID. What?

BROCCOLI. An insulting remark! So believe it or not I 'it him.

DAVID. I believe it, Mr. Smith.

BROCCOLI. And there were those three gentlemen that started my career running up. They'd never seen a blow like it. You've got talent, they said to me. So they matched me against this Dutch Martin. Him that gave me this ear, and caught me on the side of the head so that it went all milky . . . just for a moment you know, and then, when it cleared away, do you believe what I saw at the side of the ring? In the two and sixes?

DAVID. What, Mr. Smith?

BROCCOLI. The young lady and him that had passed the insulting remark. They were sitting side by side, familiar!

DAVID (*genuinely shocked*). No!

BROCCOLI. Sometimes . . . it turns out unexpected.

DAVID. Yes. . . .

BROCCOLI. But I'll meet up with Grumble. Once I'm out of here. I'll see him, down the barber's most likely. Very clean shaver was Grumble. Twice a day touch! "You've got real talent." He told me that. I saw him a year or two back. Then he had a joke with me. Oh, he was always joking. Know what he said?

DAVID. No.

BROCCOLI. He was referring to that touch I got. Over the ear, the centre of all understanding! Last time I mentioned about a job he told me, no there was nothing available. He told me it was no good. I was a doll, a paper doll from that first fight with the Dutchman. Well, it was his joke most likely . . . I've got his address somewhere. I'll call round. He'll tell me it was his joke. I was never a doll, not Broccoli!

DAVID. Of course not. . . .

BROCCOLI. You know the expression?

DAVID. Yes.

Pause. BROCCOLI *blinks and rubs his head.*

BROCCOLI. You come to say goodbye, didn't you?

DAVID. Yes, and to say . . .

BROCCOLI. Well, I enjoyed those talks we had, about the future and that. Very interesting they was.

DAVID. Yes, Mr. Smith.

BROCCOLI. But I was right, you know. It didn't come to an end, did it? I mean . . . it's still going on.

DAVID. Yes, it is.

BROCCOLI. And you said I was weak in the maths. . . .

DAVID. I misjudged you. . . .

BROCCOLI. Well. (*He looks round the room.*) I'll be off soon, to the outside. Only thing I'm likely to miss is the room.

DAVID. The room?

BROCCOLI. Peaceful in a way. Out of the main swim, of course. I liked that, being out of the swim. Quietly . . . up here.

DAVID. I expect you're busy.

BROCCOLI. It's the room I'll regret, that's all.

He looks round the room, dejected. DAVID *looks at him, seems to be about to say something, can't think of what to say, and goes.*

BROCCOLI *calls after* DAVID.

Only look out for the year three thousand, now! Don't let that catch you unawares. . . .

29. The Playground: DAVID *comes down the stairs from* BROC-
COLI'S *room and out into the playground. He crosses the playground in streaming sunshine.*

He looks guilty and dejected. A BOY *passes him running.*

DAVID. Where're you going?

BOY. It's Armstrong . . . he's got a motorized affair.

> DAVID *runs, too. They reach a* BOY *crouched over a model
> aeroplane with a small engine.*

2ND BOY. It won't work.

DAVID. Here, let me see.

> *He crouches too.*

It's the fuel. . . .

> *He makes an adjustment. With a great whirr the model
> aeroplane flies into the air. The* BOYS *straighten up.*
> DAVID *is looking, squinting against the sun at the flight of
> the plane.*
> *In the distance* BROCCOLI, *with his parcel and empty cage,
> goes out of the school gate.* DAVID *looks after him.*

BOY. Come on! She's landing. . . .

> DAVID *runs off with the other* BOYS *towards the crashing
> plane.*

Call Me a Liar

CALL ME A LIAR was first produced on BBC Television on 22 April 1958, with the following cast:

MARTHA HEINZ	*Cornell Borchers*
SAMMY NOLES	*Alec McCowan*
LANDLADY	*Rita Webb*
LADY BOARDER	*Damaris Hayman*
BUSINESS MAN	*Peter Bathurst*
PROFESSIONAL MAN	*Tony Sympson*
MR. PHEEMING	*Elwyn Brook-Jones*
MAN ON PARK BENCH	*George Benson*
DR. BOWKER	*Lionel Ngakane*
SWEDISH GIRL	*Patricia Raine*
BAR GIRL	*Ida Franklyn*
MAN IN THE BAR	*Charles Farrell*

Produced by Michael Elliott

As we fade in a street piano on a barrow is playing If You Were the Only Girl in the World *outside a row of London boarding houses in a dingy square, in the Bloomsbury or St. Pancras area.*

We see the front of a boarding house with a Room To Let *notice dangling in front of dirty lace curtains in the front window.*

1. The Hall of the Boarding House: The LANDLADY *is standing at the bottom of the stairs, shouting up.*

LANDLADY. Mr. Noles! For heaven's sake wake up, Mr. Noles. Your cereal's getting all soggy.

2. SAMMY NOLES'S *Bedroom:* SAMMY *is standing by his bed in his shirt and socks. He is lifting the mattress to extricate his trousers which he has been pressing in his sleep. He gets his trousers out and lets the mattress fall with a bump.*

In the hall the LANDLADY *reacts to the bump.*

LANDLADY. Whatever are you doing, Mr. Noles? Body-building again? You'll do yourself a nasty injury one of these days . . . body-building like that. Hurry up, Mr. Noles. You'll be late for business again.

Back in the bedroom SAMMY *is splashing water on his face at the wash-basin. In front of the wash-basin is a mirror. Beside the mirror is a motto framed on the wall. It says:*

> When You Smile
> Another Smiles.
> Start Miles
> Of Smiles.

SAMMY speaks to his face in the mirror.

SAMMY. All right, Sammy Noles. You smile at me and I'll smile at you.

The face in the mirror manages a mirthless grin.

What are you grinning at? Looking forward to today's
rise in salary? The win on the pools? Thinking of the
girl you didn't manage to fall into conversation with at
the bus stop last night? Well, she was a nice type of girl.
Nice types of girls don't fall into conversation. Not at bus
stops. (*The face in the mirror looks depressed.*) Smile, can't
you? Look, supposing we go to the pictures tonight . . . just
you and me. Well, I know we've seen everything locally.
Suppose I give you a treat. Up the West End.

*He puts on his coat and waistcoat which are hanging inside
each other on the back of a chair. The face in the mirror is
solemn.*

Oh, stop looking so gloomy. I mean, who wants to go to the
pictures with *you*?

*He combs his hair, brushes the shoulders of his coat with his
hands.*

Look, the sun's shining. It's Wednesday. Maybe we'll skip
out of the office early. Have a nice sit down in the park.
LANDLADY (*shouting, off*). *Mister* Noles!
SAMMY (*by way of final encouragement to himself in the mirror*).
Come on . . . cheer up. It may *never* happen. Go down
looking like that and those boarders'll think you've buried
your grandmother. You don't want them to start feeling
sorry for you, do you? Don't let them get *sympathetic*. . . .

3. The Boarding House Passage: SAMMY *is coming downstairs.
He still looks gloomy. Suddenly, at the dining-room door he
shoots his cuffs, pulls down his waistcoat and fixes an over-
powering smile.*

4. The Boarding House Dining-Room: Three boarders sitting

*round a table. One dreary-looking elderly man peering over the
luscious front page pin-up on the* Daily Mirror. *One precise,
ageless young man with the* Daily Telegraph. *One woman in
a cardigan reading the advertisements in* The Lady.

SAMMY NOLES *comes in, dressed, in a white stiff collar,
shiny blue suit, R.A.F. tie. He pushes away his cornflakes and
tries to light a small cigarette. His lighter, which is part of his
cigarette case, doesn't function.*

*As he speaks, the other boarders make no reaction except for an
occasional, doubting comment.*

SAMMY. Can't face it after last night. Were we out on the
town last night! Business contacts from the North of England. You know what business contacts from the North are!
They want to see it *all* (*North Country imitation*). "We're
in your hands, Sammy . . . take us where the girls are
numerous and the membership's under two shillings a
year." Bit of luck. Sammy knows his Wardour Street.

THE LADY BOARDER. Mr. Noles!

SAMMY. I haven't shocked you, Miss Evans, darling?

THE LADY BOARDER. When I passed your room at nine-
thirty on the way to retiring . . .

SAMMY (*gallant*). Why pass, Miss Evans?

THE LADY BOARDER. The light was on. I made sure you were
in there cleaning your teeth. . . .

She smiles sweetly. The other boarders look at SAMMY *with
hostility. He looks utterly destroyed, and then goes on
pleadingly.*

SAMMY. Mistaken . . . some mistake, I do assure you . . .
Half past nine-thirty? Just the very hour when I was
downing my third Sheffield United. Any of you boys ever
sampled a Sheffield United? Stout and brandy. Mixed.
Ninety per cent proof. Call me a liar? Aluminium stomachs,
these North Country contacts. One hundred per cent pure
aluminium stomachs! (*No one is impressed.*) Of course, I

take it pretty well myself. That's because I'm fit. Yogi exercises see to that. Regular yogi. You should adopt the practice, Simpson. (*The* Daily Telegraph *shudders.*) Keeps down the *avoirdupois*. Avoids the necessity for a surgical support. Promotes spiritual thoughts. A wise man of the East told me that one. One of the things I learnt with the R.A.F. in Burma. . . .

DAILY MIRROR BOARDER. Last week you learnt it in India. . . .

DAILY TELEGRAPH BOARDER. When you were in Tanks. . . .

THE LADY BOARDER. Or was it during your five years in the Navy? . . .

DAILY TELEGRAPH BOARDER. Before or after that little hush-hush trip you did for the Ministry of Information?

> SAMMY *looks from face to face, trapped; then desperately at his watch.*

SAMMY. Five to, and business beckons. Nice to natter with you, dear people, but it's out of the question. Business calls and, Holy Smoke, is there a plateful in front of me today . . . I don't know about you men, but Sammy Noles is about getting ulcers with the plateful of foreign commerce ahead of one these days. Are you finding the same headache, Simpson?

DAILY TELEGRAPH BOARDER. Lloyd's of London does maintain *some* contacts abroad. . . .

SAMMY. What about us, then? What about us? We just about have it all. Call me a liar, if you like, but it's foreign contacts all the time. Italian, Spanish, French, Swedish, Swiss . . . Foreign contacts, did you say? Only just about all the time. . . .

5. *The Office: There is a glass door with writing on it:*

The H. F. Pheeming Continental Domestic Agency.

Genuine Mothers' Helps in continuous supply.

HILARY PHEEMING, Proprietor.

In very small letters at the bottom:

Clerk: Samuel Noles.

Behind this and inside the office MR. HILARY PHEEMING, *the proprietor of the agency, is interviewing a* GIRL.

PHEEMING *is a fat, unpleasant-looking man, sitting at his desk smoking a pipe. Large photographs of his wife and children are on the desk.*

The GIRL *is sitting on a hard chair. She is blonde, young and beautiful, but with her expression of sadness, and the obvious poverty of her shoes, coat and handbag, this fact could be overlooked.*

PHEEMING. I'm very wounded by this happening. Very wounded indeed. I've found you a very ideal situation. Most of my girls would have given up two English lessons a week for a very ideal situation like that. (*The* GIRL *nods miserably.*) S.W. as well. I mean *S.*W. My girls think of S.W. as the cream de la cream. I look on your attitude, quite frankly, as an *abuse of hospitality.*

GIRL. I don't mind hard working . . .

PHEEMING. Fussy, it seems to me. Mrs. Cardew! Graciousness itself. We've stocked her with mothers'-helps ever since she first expected. Don't tell me the Colonel kissed you. . . .

GIRL. Colonel Cardew was very correct.

PHEEMING. Only what I thought. Sent an Italian girl there once. Unbalanced type of girl. Spiritualist. Came out with some slander about Colonel Cardew kissing her in the night-nursery. Didn't believe a word of it. Probably furious because she *wasn't* kissed. (*He laughs.*) You know these Neapolitans. Is that what's eating you ? . . .

The GIRL *shakes her head.*

(*Furiously.*) Look, Miss . . .

GIRL. Heinz. Martha Heinz.

PHEEMING. Where do you spring from?

GIRL. Eastern Berlin.

PHEEMING. Well, you wouldn't get it there, would you? A well-stocked table. Afternoon tea as one of the family. Television. Own room. And in S.*W*. A postal district patronized by Royalty. . . .

GIRL. It was the children.

PHEEMING. The little kids. . . .

GIRL. They were . . . brutal.

PHEEMING. What?

GIRL. The little boy was fat. Like a chief of police. And the girl . . .

PHEEMING. Delightful children.

GIRL. . . . bit me.

PHEEMING. In fun?

GIRL. No, Mr. Pheeming. (*Intensely serious.*) For political reasons, I think.

PHEEMING. Nonsense. They're delightful children. Quite delightful. All children are delightful. I won't have a word said against children. That's my own little brood. (*He shows the photographs on his desk.*) Little monkeys sometimes, as we know. But angels at heart. All children are angels at heart.

GIRL. Those children hated me. . . .

PHEEMING. It's nonsense. Now look, I'd advise you to be satisfied with your situation. The authorities may not give you a permit. Anyway, my clerk deals with this. I've a consignment of Spanish cooks arriving at Waterloo . . . My clerk should be here. (*He yells.*) Noles!

> SAMMY NOLES *steps neatly in at the door, his hat behind his back. He throws it unostentatiously on to the hat stand.*

What the devil kept you? Family again. . . .

SAMMY. Afraid so. Up all night with the youngest. . . .

PHEEMING. Teething?

SAMMY. The worry is we just don't know, Chief. Had the quack in this morning. That's why I missed my train. He's afraid she may have *swallowed something*.

PHEEMING (*gulps*). That's bad.

SAMMY. Depends on what she's swallowed. Of course, the missus is terribly cut up.

PHEEMING. She would be. It was only last week the other one broke his leg, wasn't it?

SAMMY. Climbing a tree. Boys will be . . .

PHEEMING. I thought he fell off a bus. . . .

SAMMY. Well, in a way . . . I mean, he was taking a bus on his way to climb a tree, if you see what I mean. Little devil.

PHEEMING. But delightful children. (*Dubiously.*) They *are* delightful children, aren't they, Noles?

SAMMY. Very ordinary kids, no doubt. Not oil paintings . . . Not geniuses. But the missus and I . . . *We* think the world of them.

PHEEMING. There you are, a family man. I'd only employ a family man. Bachelors? They're all shirkers! Afraid of responsibility!

SAMMY (*deprecatingly*). Well, not all . . .

PHEEMING. I'm afraid so. And I'm afraid that applies to Miss Heinz as well. From *Eastern* Berlin, you see. And she can't get on with kids. Not the type for us, I'm afraid to say. Not up to Help-U standards.

> The GIRL *looks miserable.* SAMMY, *plucking up all his small courage, comes to her rescue.*

SAMMY. Well now, Chief, some of those S.W. kids, let's admit it, they can be treacherous.

PHEEMING. They can tell by instinct. If a girl isn't sound mother's-help material . . . if she shows she's afraid of the

L.H.—I

work or them. They're like dogs in that respect . . . they
react to the smell of fear.

GIRL. I can work . . .

SAMMY. I'm sure you can, Miss . . .

PHEEMING. Don't waste too much time on this particular
case, Noles!

SAMMY. If she wants a job surely we're in duty bound . . .

PHEEMING. Not if she leaves a good place.

SAMMY. I believe I can get it sorted out.

PHEEMING. You'd better have it sorted out before I get back.
I must be at Waterloo . . .

SAMMY (*encouragingly*). Yes, you must be at Waterloo.

PHEEMING. Before my twenty Spaniards get pinched by the
coffee bars. Know what those coffee bar bastards are doing
now? Waiting on the platforms to welcome the girls with a
pair of tight trousers and nine pounds a week. Not family
men, Noles. No sense of responsibility. Bachelors, every
one of them. (*He goes out.*)

SAMMY. So long, Chief.

> SAMMY *sits at* PHEEMING'S *desk. He becomes important.*
> *The boss. He pours himself a glass of water, drops a tablet in*
> *it, stirs it with a pencil and drinks.*

GIRL. Thank you . . . you're kind.

SAMMY. That's all right. Don't let yourself get pushed
around. Now, I can't promise you anything, of course. . . .

GIRL. I only want a situation. I have first-class language,
having read English books, *Lamb's Tales*, *Water Babies*,
Forever Amber. . . .

SAMMY. Were we on the town last night?

GIRL. On the . . . ?

SAMMY (*winks*). Beating it up . . . Theatre crowd mostly.
You know what they are.

GIRL. Are they?

SAMMY. There's a little place off Wardour Street, I happen to

know. Just a piano. Members only. Small place. If you ever
find yourself there, mention my name. Ask for Sammy
Noles. I'll buy you a drink. . . .

GIRL. What would your wife say?

SAMMY. My wife?

GIRL. Yes. Your wife. . . .

SAMMY. Oh, my wife . . . Well—she's used to it by now.
What I say is: you can catch a man, but you can't build a
cage for him. Not Sammy Noles. No cage bird, Sammy.
Hang on a minute. Shocking pressure of business here to-
day. (*Answering the telephone. Suddenly in a posh voice.*)
Help-U-Continental . . . *At* your service . . . Oh, yes,
Mrs. Cardew. Well, we're all very distressed by it here. Very
distressed. Mr. Pheeming is personally most distressed.
Well, I'll talk to her, Mrs. Cardew. I'll certainly talk to her.
Call me a liar if I don't. I'm sure she'll go back to you. Call
me a liar . . .

The GIRL *shakes her head violently.*

(*Into the telephone.*) Oh, dear. No. Tut . . . tut . . . tut
. . . (*To* GIRL.) She says she won't have you back. (*To
telephone.*) Was she now? (*To* GIRL.) She says you're a Communist. (*To telephone.*) Yes, of course it did. We can quite
see that. Very embarrassing for the little nipper. (*To* GIRL.)
She says it embarrassed the little boy. Having a Communist
meet him at his infant school. Made him shunned in Kensington Gardens . . .

GIRL. I ran away from the Communists.

SAMMY (*to telephone*). She says she ran away from the Communists, Mrs. Cardew.

GIRL. In a coal train.

SAMMY (*to telephone*). In a coal train.

GIRL. Hidden by the sacks.

SAMMY (*to* GIRL). The sacks?

GIRL. The coal sacks.

L.H.–I*

SAMMY. Anyway, she doesn't want you. (*To telephone.*) Well, Mrs. Cardew, I have two nice Lithuanians here. They're friends. (*Opening a file.*) At least, I think they're friends. Colonel Cardew'll want a photograph. (*To* GIRL.) Amorous old . . . (*To telephone.*) Well, I've a photo here. Well, we're not picking them for the chorus, are we now? But they look nice, solid girls. Good pair of thick necks to them. Hardly the type what will require evenings off. Certainly, Mrs. Cardew. We'll send you particulars. By return. Thank you, Mrs. Cardew. (*He puts down phone.*) Silly cow.

GIRL. I must find a post.

SAMMY. Well, it won't be too easy. The Ministry don't like you changing, you know. And Mrs. Cardew won't reference you. That's for certain. Pheeming's pretty sore with you, and I see your permit expires . . .

The GIRL *gets up sadly to go. The telephone rings.*

SAMMY (*comforting*). This may be something . . . (*In a posh voice.*) Help-U-Continental.

He sticks a cigarette in his mouth and jabs at it with his ineffectual lighter.

(*To telephone.*) I'm sorry to hear that, sir. Very upsetting for you. Well, we haven't much on our books right now. But I'll take the particulars. (*To* GIRL.) There's a bank manager with nine children in Isleworth. His wife's just been certified insane. Does that attract you?

The GIRL *looks hopeless.*

(*To the telephone.*) Oh . . . we'll be calling you. (*He puts the telephone down.*) He wants an Italian. Says they're more used to large families.

As the GIRL *gets up to go,* SAMMY *stops her as the telephone rings again.*

Let's hope this is it . . . (*He listens, purring into the telephone.*) Of course I understand . . . Someone to look after your little boy when you're at the theatre . . . And when you don't want to dash home after the theatre . . . And when you're asleep all day. I quite understand . . . Well, I mix with a lot of theatricals, believe you me. What's the show? I can't miss that. I'll just scrawl it down. *Parisian Panty Mime.* Very neat, that . . . *Double entendre* . . . You want a French girl? (*His eyes go up in mock despair.*) Well, they are more gayer as a general rule, aren't they? . . . More "*sympathetique*" . . . We'll suit you, Miss . . . Oh, Madam, of course. So long, dear. (*He rings off.*)

GIRL. Not for me?

SAMMY *shakes his head.*

SAMMY. No point in your hanging about here now. I'll let you know if anything suitable arises.

GIRL. I should come back?

SAMMY. Yes. All right. If you like.

GIRL. What time?

SAMMY. Make it about three. I may not be back in the office till three. You know, these heavy business lunches. They're a curse really.

GIRL (*leaving*). Thank you, once again.

SAMMY. Quite a pleasure, I'm sure.

The door closes. SAMMY *raises his glass of Alka Seltzer as a toast to her disappearing figure, and drains it.*

6. *The Gardens: In the Embankment Gardens the trees are in spring leaf and big office blocks tower in the background.*

On the benches TYPISTS *and* OFFICE BOYS *are making love; elderly* CLERKS *are reading books and eating sandwiches.* TRAMPS *are sleeping in bundles of rags.*

At the refreshment kiosk, SAMMY *is buying a cardboard cup of coffee.*

On the bench to which SAMMY *comes, an elderly* MAN *is read-ing a large book and eating voraciously from a battered attaché case. He reacts with disbelief, boredom and disgust to the scene which takes place on the other end of this bench between* SAMMY *and the* GIRL.

SAMMY *arrives, sits on the bench. He puts his coffee down and takes a packet of sandwiches out of his pocket and begins to eat with small, neat gestures. He makes clucking noises with his tongue and throws crumbs to a bird.*

The GIRL *passes.* SAMMY *looks up with consternation and embarrassment.*

GIRL. Oh. Hello. . . .

SAMMY (*with forced jocularity*). Hullo, there.

GIRL. Mind if I sit down?

SAMMY. It's free.

GIRL (*smiling*). You said you had to eat a big lunch with busi-ness men.

SAMMY. Well. That is, I . . .

GIRL (*smiling more*). It was not quite true, what you said in the office.

SAMMY (*hurt*). Well. Call me a liar, but . . .

GIRL. I wouldn't do that.

SAMMY. As a matter of fact, I had a big lunch arranged but I . . . well, I cut out of it. We had a bit of sun today. It's healthier to eat in the sun . . . Wise man of the East told me that one, as it so happens . . . Here. Have a sand-wich. . . .

GIRL. You couldn't spare one?

SAMMY. That's all right. Cheese spread on the left . . . To-mato on the right . . . My landlady does them up rather tasty. . . .

GIRL. Is that what you call your wife? . . .

SAMMY. What?

GIRL. Landlady. . . .

SAMMY (*laughing desperately*). Ho! Ho! Yes. Landlady. Leader

of the Opposition. Ball and Chain. Trouble and Strife. I call
her worse than that. Bless her heart.

GIRL. She would be in a rage if she knew your sandwich, cut
with so much love, was given to a German girl in the park?

SAMMY. She's broad-minded, I told you. Served in the
W.R.N.S.

GIRL (*eating*). How was that?

SAMMY. Women's Navy. Torpedoed *three* times.

GIRL. She's a kind of hero then, your wife.

SAMMY (*modestly*). You might say so. Actually we met when I
was at sea. It's quite a story. . . .

GIRL (*not encouraging him*). I'm sure . . . I must find another
family.

SAMMY. You shouldn't have left the Colonel's. That's when
you made your big error.

GIRL. I couldn't stay there, Mr. Noles.

SAMMY. You know my name?

GIRL. I heard it in the office.

SAMMY. No reason why you shouldn't call me Sammy. People
habitually call me Sammy.

GIRL. I couldn't stay.

SAMMY. We class it as an AI situation. . . .

GIRL. I wanted to make them be happy, those children. I ran
the bath for them. Deep water, hot. And the soap so big,
shaped like a soldier in a . . . busby hat. And the towels so
pink and big. A lovely bathroom. "Come to bath," I said.
"Bath time now." But they don't move. For half an hour
they don't move. The water is cooling. "Come, please come
to bath," I implore of them. But they are still in their overcoats. The ones with velvet collars. "Come," I beg them
both and I squeak the rubber duck. Then the boy looks at
me. Small eyes. Fat face. I have a real fear of that boy. Most
of what he speaks I don't understand, but then I understand
him. "Shut up," he says. "Do you think we take orders
from bloody krauts." The mother heard him. I think she

was laughing. I was three years old when the war started, Mr. Noles. Do you think I started it?

SAMMY (*gesturing hopelessly*). I don't know.

GIRL. I don't think I did.

SAMMY. Well, there you are, and you certainly took a risk changing your job like that . . . What with the permit situation tricky as we know it is. What'll you do if we can't place you? Go back to your family?

GIRL. I can't go back. And my family . . .

SAMMY. Yes.

GIRL. Well . . . that's impossible.

SAMMY. Why? You may have to, if we can't get you suited, that is.

GIRL. I have nobody. To tell you the truth.

SAMMY. No family?

The GIRL *shakes her head.*

No one at all?

GIRL. It happens often.

SAMMY. What happens?

GIRL. Well, you know. Bombing.

SAMMY. The war?

GIRL. I was lucky, myself.

SAMMY. Lucky?

GIRL. I was in hospital. The others, mother, father, uncle, two sisters, were all at home.

SAMMY (*fingering his tie*). We did that? . . .

GIRL. I think so.

SAMMY. It's a funny thing . . . (*Speaking with great effort.*) My father had a newspaper shop. Small place in the New Kent Road. Plenty of free comics for us. Posters of all the murders out on Sundays, a few bottles of sweets for the kids. Stationery for those addicted to the writing of letters. . . .

The GIRL *looks at him curiously. His voice has changed and he is telling the truth.*

1944 and I came back from the North of England. Evacuated to an auntie, I had been previously. Doodlebug had ripped that little shop out like a rotten tooth. Rest of the family gone with it. . . .

GIRL. *We* did that?

SAMMY (*nods*). It's a . . . story I don't tell to many.

GIRL. It's true!

SAMMY (*almost surprised*). Yes, it's true, all right. You're the first one I've told that to for . . . for a long time. Since the war you . . . ?

GIRL. I worked in some factories. Then I came away in the coal train . . . A home is what I'm really looking for. . . .

SAMMY. Difficult to find? . . .

GIRL. That's why I came to Victoria Station. In the fog. And there was the Colonel Cardew to meet me. Such a funny man, laughing. Coughing. With a tweed hat. . . .

SAMMY. Another sandwich?

GIRL. You're kind. . . .

SAMMY (*deprecatingly*). Not all that kind.

GIRL. "*Gutten* afternoon," the Colonel said. "*Mein Fräulein.*" He laughed. All the way back in the car he was laughing. I thought: Here is my Uncle Max. Alive again. Silly man. But he stopped laughing as soon as we got to Kensington. . . .

SAMMY. His home?

GIRL. "You better go to your club now," his wife told him. "While I take Martha to her room. Remember the Spaniard." After that he was forbidden to speak to me. And I saw the children at the top of the stairs. Both pale. Like judges. Watching us. We were all frightened in that Kensington. Me, the Colonel, the children. We feared the others might denounce us to the madam! It wasn't a home I'd found there. This bench is most like home.

SAMMY. Here?

GIRL. And you giving me this . . . lunch.

SAMMY. That's not much. Sammy Noles can do better than

this. In the entertainment line. One day I'll sit you down to entertainment. With a knife and fork. . . .

GIRL. I don't need so much entertainment. Only a family. Like you have.

SAMMY. Oh, like me? Of course. Oh, it's a bit of a tie. Better than being lonely. You're the lonely type, strikes me.

GIRL. Silly to complain. I've got a girl friend. On Thursdays we go to the Foreign Languages Club, Bayswater. You know this club?

SAMMY. Can't say it's one of my most perpetual haunts.

GIRL. We go there for apple strudel. Coffee. Dancing to the radiogram on Thursdays.

SAMMY. Sounds pretty . . . interesting.

GIRL. Oh, yes. My girl friend and I . . . we dance all right together.

SAMMY. Together?

GIRL. Of course, we expect to meet some nice gentlemen dancers soon.

SAMMY. I haven't done much in the dancing line. Not just lately. (*Pause.*) I'd like to, of course. (*Pause.*) I mean, I might take you dancing.

GIRL. How could you?

SAMMY. Why not?

GIRL. Well . . . You're . . .

SAMMY. You mean, my family ties?

GIRL. Of course.

SAMMY. I might manage it. I'm not saying I couldn't. Look, I'm not *happily* married, you know. Don't run away with that idea. . . .

GIRL. You're not?

SAMMY. We stick it for the children, naturally. But my wife doesn't really understand me. . . .

The MAN *on the end of the bench sighs at this with deep disapproval. The* GIRL *looks sympathetic.*

GIRL. She doesn't?

SAMMY. Very good-looking girl, of course. But intensely practical, you know. Washing machine minded. Now I'm more the poetic type. I mean, I like *music*.

The MAN *on the end of the bench can't stand this.*

GIRL. Do you like it?

SAMMY. Well, not all music perhaps. But a little music, in moderation, I like. So I might slip over to that club of yours . . . say . . .

GIRL. Yes?

SAMMY. Next Thursday?

GIRL. Only if you can. Perhaps it would be wrong. . . .

SAMMY. I *will* come. Call me a liar if I don't. I'll tell the wife . . .

The MAN *on the bench is shocked by* SAMMY'S *intended deception.*

I'll tell her I've got to go out on a job. Well, that'll be true, won't it? Almost true.

GIRL (*thoughtfully*). Almost true. . . .

SAMMY (*looks at his watch*). Well, so long for now. Business presses. . . .

He gets up and leaves her, waving. Then he struts off, self-confident, on the balls of his feet, past the benches of tramps and lovers.
The GIRL, *left alone, clicks her tongue and throws the crumbs of* SAMMY'S *sandwiches to the birds.*

GIRL (*to herself*). So long for now. . . .

The MAN *on the bench can no longer contain himself. He leans over and speaks confidentially to the* GIRL.

MAN. That's the sort of thing that's going to bring Western civilization crumbling to the ground.

GIRL. I'm sorry. I don't understand.

MAN (*an obsessed glint in his eye*). Married men, larking about! That's what did for Babylon. History informs us. And Ancient Rome. And the Pharaohs. Look here. I happen to have made the Pharaohs of Egypt my special study. What's written on the middle pyramid? You don't know.

GIRL shakes her head.

There's not many Regius Professors know it either. But I've made that particular pyramid my full-time reading. "Married Men, Oh Kings . . ." it quite clearly states . . . "must stay with their wives!"

A CHILD *runs by and falls over. The* GIRL *is about to pick it up when a young* MOTHER *picks it up possessively. The* FATHER *swings the* CHILD *on to his shoulders. They walk away together, the* FATHER *and* MOTHER *holding hands, the* CHILD *on the* FATHER'S *shoulders. The* GIRL *looks after them longingly.*
Over a close-up of the GIRL'S *face, the* MAN *speaks off-screen.*

Take the example of Ancient China. Just look what happened to that!

7. SAMMY'S *Bedroom:* SAMMY *is standing in front of the mirror combing his hair.*
We see the back of his head and his face in the mirror.

He is making speeches to himself.
The piano is playing in the street outside.

SAMMY. My Lords, Ladies and Gentlemen, My Lord Archbishop, Mr. Prime Minister . . . My Lords the Commissioners of Inland Revenue . . . I will now call upon Lord Noles, K.G.V.O., M.C., to give his usual brilliant summing up of the Company's position. Pray silence, My Lords.

Lord Noles . . . (*He whistles and combs his hair.*) Now here is a pleasant little duty. As chairman and managing director of Help-U-Continental, I take great pleasure in making this small presentation to a humble, often forgotten employee . . . Not very bright, perhaps, but a tireless plodder. A real old cart-horse from the Stamping Department. My faithful old clerk, Pheeming. This handsome . . . set of golf balls . . . Don't cry, Pheeming. You poor old wreck. We all know you're long past golf . . . (*He sings to himself in the mirror, conversationally.*) Going out tonight, Sammy? Makes all the difference, doesn't it? (*In his speech-making voice.*) And I take particular pleasure in announcing that, owing to the enormous turnover of foreign girls this summer, we declare a sumptuous dividend. Thank you, Your Royal Highness. My Lord Archbishop.

He goes to the window, opens it and throws out some money to the MUSICIAN.

Good luck, Charlie.

MUSICIAN (*looking up, surprised*). Good luck to you.

Combing his hair, SAMMY *combs the front of it down into a Hitler forelock. When he does this he makes a short Hitler speech in phoney German.*

SAMMY. Und der spastic und der climans der her life for amicht Sammy Noles gersprecken. (*He combs back his hair.*) She was only three when it all started. Not her fault. Poor little . . . Now really, Sammy, mind your language. Well, she's pretty, isn't she . . . For a night out. No need to get involved. No need to ever see her again . . . Leave her after the last waltz. . . .

He hums a waltz. Then murmurs in a thick, broken accent.

My darling, we may not have very long together. Fate may have bitterness in store for us. Our paths may not cross again. Do not cry . . . My little edelweiss. Fate is not too

unkind to us. She has given us a last gift . . . This waltz
. . . (*Crescendo humming.*) Excuse me, please. Yes, Fritz,
what is it? I said no interruptions. (*Saluting.*) Sir. Last
night . . . What's that? Some fool's thrown a bomb at the
Archduke, Sir. My God. Do you realize what this means,
my darling . . . *It means war.*

The door opens. The LANDLADY *comes in with the trousers
she's been ironing.*

LANDLADY. Were you talking to someone, Mr. Noles?

SAMMY. Just . . . talking.

LANDLADY (*mystified*). I quite understand. Look, I've given
you real knife edges.

SAMMY. It's very kind. . . .

LANDLADY. Well, you don't often go out for an evening, do
you, Mr. Noles?

SAMMY. Only when the pleasure takes me, nowadays. I'm
choosy in my old age. Now this one tonight . . .

LANDLADY. The opposite sex?

SAMMY. Bet your life!

LANDLADY. Not one of these nasty foreign girls, I hope, like
you read about in the papers.

SAMMY. Of course not . . . Real English rose this one.
Mannequin.

LANDLADY. Whatever . . .

SAMMY. You'll see her posed, one of these fine days. Slap on
the cover of one of your fashion books, with her eyebrows
hitting the ceiling and her lips ready to suck at a straw and
her little round box of tricks for carrying about in the tube.
(*He makes a model girl face, putting on his trousers.*) And maybe me in a bowler hat, all misty in the background. Real
class, you see. Only real class does Sammy nowadays. . . .

LANDLADY. Let's hope she's a nice girl. Underneath it all.

SAMMY (*suddenly serious*). Oh yes. She certainly is . . . a
nice girl.

He puts on his coat, gives a final flourish with his comb, and goes out of the door past the LANDLADY.

LANDLADY (*from the top of the stairs*). I'd like to see you settled, Mr. Noles. Really, I would. I'd like to see you married. . . .

SAMMY goes down the stairs and out of the front door, her words echoing behind him.
As he hears them he looks surprised, puzzled and finally pleased as he walks out into the street.

8. *The Foreign Languages Club, Bayswater: A crowd of people are by the radiogram at the end of a long room: an* INDIAN GIRL *and various* GIRLS *and* MEN, *including two* AFRICANS *and a tall* FINNISH GIRL.
The GIRL *is standing by the wall. She is looking anxiously at the people coming into the Club.*
One of the AFRICANS *is looking at the* GIRL, *and starts to speak to her.*

AFRICAN. Excuse. I am Dr. Bowker. The London School of Economics.

The GIRL *hasn't noticed him. She is looking at the door.*

Dr. Bowker, please.
GIRL. I'm sorry.
AFRICAN. It is gay here tonight. Soon the radiogram will be in use, I am told.
GIRL. Yes.

SAMMY comes in, looking lost. The GIRL *waves to him. He waves brightly, and joins her and the* AFRICAN.

AFRICAN. Ah. You have a companion?
GIRL. Mr. Noles.
AFRICAN. I am Dr. Bowker. The London School of Economics.

SAMMY. Evening, Doc. Delighted to meet you, I'm sure.

AFRICAN (*thoughtfully*). Now that is a curious intonation in your voice. Not English. Not English surely?

SAMMY. Funny you should say that. Now my father . . .

Music starts from the radiogram.

GIRL. You see. There is to be music. . . .

AFRICAN. I told you.

SAMMY. I was mentioning about my father, Doc. You see, in Cornwall, where he happens to be very well known—

GIRL. Shall we dance?

SAMMY. A very well-known character, all over that Duchy. All my family are there. Cornwall? I know it like the back of my hand.

GIRL (*persistent*). Please. Let's dance.

SAMMY. All right. Excuse us, Doc.

The AFRICAN *bows. The music is a waltz.* SAMMY *and the* GIRL *dance. The following dialogue takes place while* SAMMY *and the* GIRL *do a slow waltz together.*

What's the matter? You look depressed.

GIRL. I am.

SAMMY. Your job?

GIRL. No. You.

SAMMY. Me?

GIRL. I thought you told me the truth.

SAMMY. Call me . . . What about?

GIRL. Your family. The shop they had . . . Hit . . .

SAMMY. Course I did.

GIRL. Then why all that story about Cornwall?

SAMMY. There must be some mistake.

GIRL (*depressed*). Yes . . . and I thought we were the same. It had happened to both of us.

They dance in silence. Then SAMMY *says, with a great effort:*

SAMMY. It's just the way I talk. Other people make me do it, really.

GIRL. Other people?

SAMMY. When he said that—about my voice, well I could just see my father . . . in Cornwall. And the old stone farm-house. Yellow fields and the blue sea. A place to take you for a summer holiday . . . Look, maybe I could ask him to send you up some cream!

GIRL. But it's not true.

SAMMY. It seems true when I say it. Anyway, life would be ever so monotonous, wouldn't it—if you couldn't well . . . exaggerate a bit . . . sometimes?

GIRL. Monotonous?

SAMMY. Well. I honestly mean dull.

GIRL. Today's not dull. Today's really happening.

SAMMY. Yes, today. Trouble is, there aren't so many like it.

They dance a little while in silence. The music stops. They go and stand against the wall.

GIRL. In Notting Hill Gate . . . in my new situation . . . my girl-friend has found me . . . it is always raining. The gentleman is a dentist . . . His chair is in the front room. His visitors are all sad people. The lady does not confide in me. Monday, Tuesday, Wednesday—no letters drop through the door. The little child—such thin arms—seems full of sorrow. Then Thursday. Today, it stops raining. The lady has a home perm. Her hair looks like burnt grass. And then she is singing. It is not much, her voice. Tinny. But it's something. And I bump into the dentist coming out of his surgery and he laughs at me. And the child . . . when I put the child to bed, I feel cold thin arms locked round my neck like a chain. "Don't ever leave us," this child says. "Don't ever go." And when I come out into the street there's no rain. The days change sometimes. Now I feel happy.

SAMMY. You do?

GIRL. And you?

SAMMY. Of course. I talked when I was getting ready. And I sang too. (*Conscience-stricken.*) But I told someone you were a model.

GIRL. A what?

SAMMY. Like on the fashion books with their snowdrop faces and eyebrows like someone who's just had a jab at the hypodermic. (*He makes a model's face.*) Silly part—I don't want that type of girl at the best of times.

GIRL (*laughing*). Who did you say that to—your wife?

SAMMY. I was forgetting her. . . .

GIRL. I suppose it is dreadful, for us to forget her. . . .

SAMMY. I suppose. . . .

GIRL. If she loves you. . . .

SAMMY. She doesn't care, out at a whist drive most likely . . . cocktails . . . whist drives . . . living it up with the smart set. That's all she cares about it. . . .

Another tune has started. The GIRL *and* SAMMY *dance off slowly together. After a pause the* GIRL *says:*

GIRL. I don't believe in your wife . . . When I dance I don't believe there's anyone else in the world. Just me and . . . it's not dull at all.

SAMMY *is frightened by this fact, and begins to do an imitation.*

SAMMY (*in his foreign accent*). Fate may have bitterness in store for us. Our paths may not cross again. Do not cry, my little edelweiss.

The GIRL *is laughing at him.*

GIRL. You're so *funny.*

SAMMY (*sadly*). Yes. I suppose I am. . . .

GIRL. You don't meet many funny people. Not as a mother's help.

The record is changed and the music becomes slow and passionate jazz. A dark hand taps SAMMY'S *shoulder. It is the* AFRICAN.

SAMMY. What is it, Fritz? I thought I said no interruptions.
AFRICAN. May I have the pleasure?

The GIRL *smiles reluctantly. The* AFRICAN *leads her into an immediate slow jive.* SAMMY *is seized by the* FINN. *She whirls him into an involved dance. The following dialogue takes place with a short* SAMMY *being breathlessly whisked round this strong and statuesque* FINN.

SAMMY. Are you a mother's help, too?
FINN. Believe me, little friend, where I work the mothers help me!
SAMMY. They do?
FINN. My present situation brings me tea in bed. What does she need help for anyway? In Finland the mothers are more sturdy. . . .
SAMMY. I'm sure. . . .
FINN. You're a good little dancer.
SAMMY. You think so?
FINN. A fine sense of rhythm.
SAMMY (*modest*). Nothing special.
FINN. You should come here more often. You and I (*She clutches him close to her.*) fit so well together.
SAMMY. The fact is . . . I can't come here as often as one might like . . . A . . . married man . . . like me . . . has ties.
FINN (*flinging him out at arm's length*). Married!
SAMMY. I'm afraid so.
FINN. Then you're no use to us.
SAMMY. What?
FINN. No good here at all.
SAMMY. What do you mean?
FINN. No help. You understand?

SAMMY. No. What are you girls after?

FINN. You don't know?

SAMMY. Haven't any idea.

FINN. Mothers' helps! That's what the regulations make us
. . . Do you think we like it?

SAMMY. One hardly assumes so.

FINN. Look, my little friend . . . No girl here is looking for
a situation. You know what they are searching for?

SAMMY. What?

FINN. *Husbands.*

> SAMMY *flinches and is then whirled round under a dominat-
> ing arm.*

Any man. Any small, mean man with a British passport. Any
liar, thief, no-good. We'd beat him up. Swallow him . . .
We'd marry him! Then—no need for being a mother's help
. . . Any little bit of a man . . . To give us our nation-
ality. . . .

> *The record stops, changes to a sentimental dance tune.*
> SAMMY *is released. He sees the* GIRL *move towards him.*

GIRL. Are you happy here tonight?

SAMMY. Yes, that is, I . . .

GIRL. Shall we dance again—

> SAMMY *looks at her with sudden suspicion and then in despair
> looks at his watch.*

SAMMY. Well, the truth of the matter is . . .

GIRL. You're tired of dancing? Perhaps you don't like this
club?

SAMMY. No. It's just . . .

GIRL. There's a café opposite. We could eat something, perhaps. Just a quiet place. We two could slip away . . .

SAMMY (*suspicious, frightened and anxious to escape*). I must
go . . . That's right. My wife. Of course, my wife . . .

she'll be back. From the whist drive. I must go home to my
wife.

He turns from her, running. She is left, gesturing hopelessly.

9. *The Gardens:* SAMMY, *sad and lonely, is eating his sandwiches
and reading a paper. It begins to rain. For a while he doesn't
notice the rain. Then he gets up and runs to the refreshment kiosk.
Inside the kiosk he gets a cardboard cup of coffee and takes it to
drink beside the* MAN *on the bench, who is sitting gazing straight
ahead of him with a fixed expression. In this scene the* MAN *on the
bench is taking no notice of* SAMMY, *but is talking in a rapt way
to himself.*

SAMMY (*brightly*). Nasty day.

The MAN *takes no notice.*

Good day for ducks.

The MAN *still takes no notice.*

Seasonable, of course, in the spring.

The MAN *starts mumbling to himself.*

MAN. If they'd only pay attention. The Pyramid has it all
down. If only they'd stop to read it. The message is there.
Loud and clear. All you scholars of Oxford College can't
read it. But there's some that's got the point all right, across
the water.
SAMMY. Pardon?
MAN. For thirty years after the Battle of the Nations shall the
selfish triumph. Adulterers. Drinkers of strong tea and
methylated spirits. Then there shall start an outbreak of
small fires.
SAMMY. Come again?
MAN. Volume after volume published about the Pharaohs of
Egypt. They all completely missed the point.

L.H.–K

SAMMY (*solicitous*). Old chap, you don't mind me saying this, but you're in a bad way. You're talking to yourself. You ought to watch that. Comes of being too much on your own.

The MAN *takes no notice.*

It's cleared a bit. Better be getting back to work, I suppose.

Before he leaves, he pats the MAN *on the shoulder.*

You know, you ought to get out a bit. Meet a few more people. That's my advice to you.

MAN (*to himself*). Have they overlooked China?

SAMMY *walks away alone, past the wet, empty benches back to work.*

10. The Office: SAMMY *comes in and shakes out his dripping hat and hangs it up. He sits at the desk and looks bored and lonely. On an impulse he gets out a file and looks at a photograph in it. It is a crude passport photograph of the* GIRL.

SAMMY. Fancy seeing you. Where've you been all these weeks? Found him, have you, that poor sucker, with an English passport . . . ? That sawn-off, bald, damp-eyed old hundred per cent British duodenal with his teeth on the mantelpiece and his clean driving licence and no convictions known. Hooked him, have you? Register Officed him? Given him the old Love, Honour and Obey? Another four months and you'll have a love cart full of a little dribbling citizen with no teeth and a British passport. Then you'll be well fixed, won't you? They won't deport you then. Well, you didn't pin it on Sammy Noles. Oh, no. Sammy gets up too early in the morning for that little carry on. Know what they tell you in the army? Cover your line of retreat? That's my rule. I had my line of retreat well prepared. Told you I was *married already*. That stopped that lark. When I think—you nearly fooled me. Nearly fooled Sammy Noles.

SAMMY *is alone in the office. He gets out of* PHEEMING'S

chair, walks round to the front of the desk, squats on his heels, turns the photograph round and stares at it. The tension goes out of his face, which, seen from the level of the desk, relaxes.

No offence of course . . . Not that I blame you for trying . . . Not that there's any ill will . . . What've you been doing, anyway, all these long days and nights. Nothing much? Neither have I. Perhaps everyone's gone to the sea-side or some old place. I mean, they've taken the roads up and it's getting warm in the streets. If you shut your eyes you just hear flap, flap, flap, feet on the pavement. No one speaking. No one to talk to. It gets lonely, doesn't it?

He picks the photograph off the desk. He is kneeling on the floor, talking to it.

I liked you. I thought you were a real, nice type of girl. I'd like to hear from you—know how you're getting on. But you shouldn't have done it . . . You weren't being straight with me, I mean. Not telling the truth . . . That's what I didn't like. You not telling me the truth.

The door opens behind him. The GIRL *walks into the office.* SAMMY *puts the photograph into his pocket and starts searching the floor without looking up.*

Sit down, Miss . . .

GIRL. Heinz. Martha Heinz. Were you talking to someone?

SAMMY struggles to his feet.

SAMMY. Not a bit of it . . . (*He covers his retreat behind his desk.*) Just . . . making a search for something . . . Things roll from me. (*Brightly, sitting behind the desk.*) How's every little thing?

GIRL. I must have a new situation.

SAMMY. Child bit you again?

GIRL. No, this child . . . we liked each other.

Quite unexpectedly she begins to cry and fumbles in her bag for a handkerchief. SAMMY *produces his handkerchief, looks at it, regretfully, decides it is too dirty and puts it back into his pocket. Meanwhile, the* GIRL *has got her handbag open, and, finding her handkerchief, blows her nose loudly. She recovers, and says:*

But the dentist's brother Edward, he came to dinner every Thursday. After dinner every Thursday he came into the kitchen. "You wash and I'll dry," he said. He was so nervous. He broke all the glasses. He became a terrible embarrassment. He asked me to marry him.

SAMMY. He asked you—what?

GIRL. To marry him. Every Thursday. I came to dread it.

SAMMY. A pity. . . .

GIRL. What?

SAMMY. He was a Pole? . . . Or Lithuanian? . . . Iti? . . . Jerry? Russian extraction?

GIRL (*shaking her head*). Solid English. Through and through.

SAMMY. Then why not?

GIRL. What?

SAMMY. Marry him?

GIRL. Why ever . . . Oh, for the passport, you mean?

SAMMY. Isn't that what you girls—

GIRL. I have heard it. (*She laughs.*) I think it is rare. I couldn't love a man . . . not for his personal documents. It is too stupid. To marry for that reason . . . Would you . . . marry for a passport?

SAMMY. No, well I . . .

GIRL. I forgot. You're married already.

SAMMY. Oh yes. I was forgetting too. Well, this Edward . . . You didn't fancy him at all?

GIRL. Poor man. He was so honest. He had a face and eyes like glass. They couldn't have hidden anything.

SAMMY. A . . . decent chap?

GIRL. "I'll be quite straight with you . . ." he said. "I like
to play a little hockey on Saturdays. You won't want me to
cut that out when we're married?" "No," I had to say.
"You can carry on playing hockey. Because I'm not going
to marry you." He had no need of me . . . But the child . . .

SAMMY (*fearing tears*). Oh, dear. . . .

GIRL. A little, ugly child . . . always in trouble . . . never
played games . . . Always telling lies . . . We needed
each other . . .

SAMMY (*suddenly enthusiastic, pulling money from his pocket*).
Look, Martha, I'm flush this week. What about an evening
out? Tonight. What's better than this very night? Something on toast at the Corner House and then the upstairs of a
West End pictures? Two or three shorts before I drop you
at your very door . . .

GIRL. No, Sammy. I would like to come out with you. But it's
no good.

SAMMY. But our last dance-up. You were the very one to
suggest . . .

GIRL. It was stupid. I was so lonely . . . I shouldn't have
suggested it. It was very wrong.

SAMMY. Why ever?

GIRL. Your wife.

SAMMY. Oh, her . . . I'll tell her some story. (*Overcome by
the originality of his idea.*) I'll tell her I was kept late at the
office.

GIRL. No. We can't go on telling lies. . . .

SAMMY. We can't? But when you talked about that child
. . . its lying was rather what drew you to it. . . .

GIRL. For a child, lying is necessary. A child must protect
itself. Also where I came from you have to tell lies to avoid
death, or prison or to get food. But in England, lying is a
luxury. There's no need for it. In the end the lies would get
like the hockey on Saturdays—hard work with no meaning—
and no joy.

SAMMY. If I was to tell you . . .

GIRL. Yes. . . .

SAMMY. I wasn't really married. . . .

GIRL. I shouldn't believe it. We couldn't walk about in a dream all the time. We'd have to wake up. . . .

SAMMY. No. In that case . . .

GIRL. Tell me of another situation, please. Then I'll be moving on.

SAMMY. No. Look, Martha, I can't just be alone again. Don't leave me alone. . . .

GIRL. I don't like it either.

SAMMY. Look, there's something I've just got to explain to you. Look, that old Pheeming'll be back in a minute. I've got to talk. I've got to tell you. Look, meet me once. Just tonight. Just so I can talk to you.

GIRL. What can you say ? . . .

SAMMY. There's something. There must be something . . . Look, it's—all—got to do with . . .

> *He looks nervously at the door. There is a sound of footsteps on the stairs.*

I can't tell you now. Meet me tonight. Six p.m. I'll be through. (*He begins to write on a piece of paper.*) Eros. Pica-dilly Circus.

GIRL. Where the boy shoots the arrow . . . and the Americans look so sad.

SAMMY. I'll write it down. . . .

> *The door opens.* PHEEMING *is standing in the doorway looking suspiciously at* SAMMY. SAMMY *hands the paper to the* GIRL *in a business-like way.*

There you are, Miss Heinz. And I hope this time you'll be really suited.

11. Regent Street in the Early Evening: The GIRL *is walking aimlessly along. She is killing time and her face is reflected in the windows. It is twenty to six. She suddenly walks with more purpose towards Piccadilly.*

12. The Office: The clock on the office wall says five to six. SAMMY *and* PHEEMING *are alone in the office.*

SAMMY. Well. If you don't need me, Chief, I'd better be off.

PHEEMING (*gloomily*). Scared of the wife creating?

SAMMY. Yes, that's it. Of course that's it. You see, she's asked some people in. . . .

PHEEMING. Old cats! They'll just run you out of digestive biscuits and ask your wife why you always get on the same bus as that disgusting Mrs. Humphries. Don't I know them!

SAMMY (*laughing dutifully*). Oh, yes. Quite, perfectly so.

PHEEMING. Look here. I respect a man who respects his family. But we're not slaves, you know. We're not bloody mothers' helps. Let's go for a couple of shorts. . . .

SAMMY. No, Chief. Not tonight. . . .

PHEEMING. What's the trouble? Afraid the cats'll smell it out? Here. A cachou to suck in the tube.

SAMMY. No. That is, tonight . . . I made a promise.

PHEEMING. What's eating you, Noles? Five years you've been with me. Have I ever before shown any temptation to ask you out for a drink?

SAMMY. No, Chief. Not that I remember.

PHEEMING. Well then. For all you know it's a sign of favour— a sign that you may be going to advance in our . . . organization. Are you so stinking in the unearned income that this sort of hint means nothing to you?

SAMMY. It's very complimentary, Chief. Perhaps another night. . . .

He looks at the clock. It is six o'clock.

PHEEMING. We work pretty closely together, Noles. Things

might not be too comfortable for you in the organization if you felt I had my knife in you.

SAMMY *looks doubtful.*

I don't happen to want to go home just yet.
SAMMY. All right, Chief. A quick one. Just a very quick one.

PHEEMING *stands up. His great hand falls on* SAMMY'S *shoulder and kneads it.*

PHEEMING. Of course it'll be a quick one . . . Just one for the road. We're both family men, aren't we?
SAMMY (*miserably*). Both family men. . . .

13. Piccadilly Circus: MARTHA *and* ANOTHER GIRL *are waiting, independently, for dates. Background of some Americans on the steps of Eros.* MARTHA, *wearing a mackintosh, looks at her watch.*

14. The Drinking Club: It is a small and seedy Wardour Street drinking club. SAMMY *is drinking against time.* PHEEMING *is in a slow, expansive mood. They're alone except for the bar girl and a large, square, lonely drinker perched on a stool. The clock behind the bar says ten past six.*

PHEEMING. Well, you really sink them, don't you? . . . Have another . . . Just for the road. . . .
SAMMY. No. That is, I . . .
PHEEMING. Go on. Keep your wife waiting. What are you— a man or an alarm clock? (*He laughs.*) Hey, what do you think of that? That's rather good, isn't it? A man or an alarm clock. Someone ought to write that down. Go on, Noles. Say you were kept late at the office.
SAMMY (*shocked*). I wouldn't do that, Chief. It wouldn't be true.
PHEEMING. Have some guts, then. Tell a lie for once in your life.

15. Piccadilly Circus: The other GIRL *meets her date.* MARTHA
is still waiting.

16. The Drinking Club.
PHEEMING. Come on, dear. Another two . . . This man
  sucks them up like a vacuum cleaner.
SAMMY. No, really, I . . .
PHEEMING. Don't worry, my boy. She'll be waiting. That's
  the worst of wives. They wait for ever.

> *He puts his hand in his hip pocket, pulls out a number of
> pound notes and a dirty piece of paper which, suddenly serious
> and slightly drunk, he unfolds.*

Look at this, Noles. Here's family life for you. You'll be
getting one of them tomorrow morning, I don't doubt. Billy
doo from the wife: "Dear Mr. Pheeming, If you leave your
filthy shoes on the kitchen table once more, you fat slug, I
swear I'll put them in the boiler. Yours sincerely, Edna
Pheeming (Mrs.)"
SAMMY (*aghast*). Is *that* what it's like?

17. Piccadilly Circus: MARTHA *is looking anxiously around, and
trying to avoid the hopeful stare of a camera-slung, crew-cut*
AMERICAN *with rimless glasses.*

18. The Drinking Club: The clock says half past six. PHEEMING
is now slightly maudlin and almost tearfully confidential.
SAMMY *is desperate, but listening to* PHEEMING *with fascinated
horror.*

PHEEMING. It's just years now since Mrs. Pheeming and I
  actually said a word to each other. It was the Coronation.
  "Turn that television down," she said. "Mother's got one of
  her nasty heads." Her mother was there, *of course*. So I
  turned the television up. Well, you've got to be master in
  your household. So she turned it down. So I turned it up.

So she turned it down. "You do that once more," she said, "and I swear I'll never speak to you again." "Suits me," I said. So she never did. Just notes. Of course, after these years, the children are bound to notice something. It's so quiet, gets you down. I've no use for a bachelor. I've no use for a man who can't face up to family life.

SAMMY. It sounds horrible. . . .

PHEEMING. Oh, the kids still speak to me. They're not great scholars, my kids. Not great hands at writing.

SAMMY. Well, I really must be going.

PHEEMING (*shouts*). Stay here a minute, can't you? Don't you see? I want to *talk to someone*. Here, have another drink—

19. Piccadilly Circus: The AMERICAN *offers* MARTHA *his packet of cigarettes. She's trying her best to shrug him off.*

20. The Drinking Club: PHEEMING *is sitting on a stool, more maudlin than ever.*

PHEEMING. I was fifty-three yesterday. If I live till I'm eighty, that's another twenty-seven years we shan't converse. Of course, it's got to be faced. Family life . . . mowing the lawn. The mortgage, the schedule A . . . The fire and life policy with profits . . . You can't avoid it . . . I hate a bachelor. . . .

The clock says a quarter to seven.

SAMMY. I must get a tube, Chief.

PHEEMING. Don't turn up on time, Noles. Don't pander. Let her know who's the master of the house. If she doesn't speak to you . . . Button your lips as well. Don't give in. I hate a hen-pecked husband.

Clock strikes seven.

And when I first met her . . . Pretty as the lid on a box of biscuits. We were dancing together. Some palais.

Which I really forget. Only you, she said. You're the only one I want to talk to. So I give her the green certificate. Of course our Dorothy was well on the way. Pretty baby, too. Mother's eyes.

The telephone on the bar rings.

BAR GIRL. Mr. Pheeming. Yes. He's in here . . . For you.

PHEEMING. Dorothy. What the hell? Oh. Mrs. Pheeming found the membership card, did she? With the telephone number. Quite the Sherlock Holmes, I don't think. Well, I suppose her Gracious Majesty couldn't put her mouth to the telephone herself. Wants me home. Does she? Well, at my convenience. Tell Mrs. Pheeming that, Dorothy. At my own convenience. (*He slams down the telephone.*) I'd better go. Only . . . I'll write my wife a stinker about this when I get home. I'll burn up the notepaper! I'll be sarcastic. A real stinker. . . .

21. Piccadilly Circus: MARTHA *gives up waiting and walks away.*

22. The Drinking Club: SAMMY, *rather tight, pulls his notes out of his pocket and buys a drink.* PHEEMING *has gone. Only* SAMMY *and the* SOLITARY DRINKER *are at the bar.*

BAR GIRL. Staying, are you?

SAMMY. It's too late.

BAR GIRL. Too late to go home?

SAMMY. It's too late for everything. I mean . . . What's *in* marriage, anyway? What do people do it for? Seems I've seen you before. Not English, are you?

BAR GIRL. Wandsworth.

SAMMY. Funny, I made sure you were . . . Italian . . . I thought I saw you in Venice. Long time since I was in Venice. We fought all up that way, of course. Eighth Army.

SOLITARY DRINKER. No, you never!

SAMMY. Well, call me a liar. . . .

SOLITARY DRINKER. That's what you are. Eighth Army was never in Venice. Just shooting the line. . . .

SAMMY. Well, there must be some mistake . . . the Ninth Army.

SOLITARY DRINKER. You never was in the army! You're too young!

SAMMY. Here. You mind who you're talking to. Who are you? You big mouth.

SOLITARY DRINKER (*advancing on him*). *You bloody little liar.*

The BAR GIRL *stares.* SAMMY'S *face shows a sort of resignation. The* SOLITARY DRINKER'S *great ham-like fist comes crashing towards the camera.*

23. *The Office. The Next Morning:* PHEEMING *is talking into the telephone. The* GIRL *is sitting opposite him.*

PHEEMING. Your name isn't Mrs. Noles? You say it's Miss Doddsworth. But that's Sammy Noles's home? You're not passing as his wife. You've never been so insulted in your life . . . See here, madam . . .

He puts his hand over the mouthpiece.

Can he have been deceiving me? Enjoying himself as a single man all these years. Not married, is it? Leaving me to sweat out married life on my own? (*To telephone.*) What about the kids then? That little devil what broke his leg. (*To* GIRL.) Lying swine. Hasn't even been troubled by kids. (*To telephone.*) Never even had one kid of Noles's then?

Yelps from telephone.

All right, sue me. All right. Send me a solicitor's letter. You're chaste as a snowflake . . . Untouched by human hand . . . Virgin soil. All right, Mrs. Noles . . . Miss Doddsworth then. Oh, go and get yourself a husband! (*He bangs down the receiver.*) Lies. All lies. Made up as an excuse for being late for the office. Think of that. All that sympathy wasted. Every morning I'd ask after his wife and kids. Might as well have saved my breath. She says he's met with an accident. . . .

GIRL. An accident? Is it serious?

PHEEMING. Can't be too serious for me.

GIRL. He hasn't a situation for me.

PHEEMING. I don't know what he's got. Call him if you like. Here's the address, and telephone number. Only keep him away from me . . . (*He offers her a piece of paper.*)

GIRL (*doubtfully*). I suppose it's no use.

PHEEMING. Take it if you want it.

GIRL (*taking it reluctantly*). I shall not use it.

PHEEMING. Do what you like.

GIRL (*thoughtfully*). And he was never married at all.

PHEEMING. Think of that. . . .

During the following speech the GIRL *quietly goes out.*

A lousy irresponsible bachelor . . . Inventing himself a wife . . . and kids . . . and a mortgage . . . and a lawn mower . . . and schedule A . . . and rates . . . and a life policy with profits . . . It's amazing. I've got to tell someone. (*He telephones.*) Dorothy, is that you? Is Mother there? Look here, Dorothy! *I want to speak to Mrs. Pheeming!*

24. *The Gardens: The* GIRL, *lonely and very thoughtful, walks down a row of park benches on which lovers are sitting kissing or holding hands. She arrives at a bench, empty except for the* MAN *on the bench, and sits folding and unfolding the bit of paper with* SAMMY'S *address on it, which* PHEEMING *has given her. The* MAN *speaks, looking hard in the opposite direction.*

MAN. I'm glad to see you alone, young lady.

GIRL. Alone?

MAN. Last time it was a married man. I remember things clearly.

GIRL. Oh, yes. This was the bench.

MAN. My bench.

GIRL. Yours?

MAN (*bursting out*). Corruption. It comes to this very bench. Of course that's what finished Egypt. Civilization? Doomed.

GIRL. It was here. He gave me a sandwich. . . .

MAN. Loneliness must be faced. Days and nights speaking a lonely voice. When no one listens.

GIRL. But he was never married. . . .

MAN. Deception. We can't comfort ourselves with deception. That *was* tried, of course, in ancient China.

GIRL. He wasn't married . . . (*She comes to a decision.*) I must go. Goodbye . . . and I hope it all comes right, about civilization, I mean.

MAN (*cheerfully*). Doomed, of course. All the signs are clearly there.

> *The* GIRL *moves off. She walks between the benches. Then she begins to run.*

25. SAMMY'S *Bedroom:* SAMMY *is lying in bed. He has a bandage over one eye and a thermometer stuck in his mouth. He looks gravely concerned about his condition. He is reading a book:* Self Defence for Everyone. *The door opens. The* GIRL *enters and sits on the bed.* SAMMY *murmurs past the thermometer. He puts the book away. The* GIRL *takes the thermometer out and looks at it. She smiles and puts it on the table without reading it.*

GIRL. I think you may live.

> SAMMY *avoids her eye and looks out of the window.*

SAMMY. I let you down badly.

GIRL. Yes, you did.

SAMMY. I never had a wife.

GIRL. I know. So does Mr. Pheeming. He's very cross.

SAMMY. Oo! Christmas!

GIRL. Sammy. What have you been afraid of? So long?

SAMMY. I'm not afraid. . . .

GIRL. But those lies. . . .

SAMMY. You're right. I was afraid. I didn't like to tell . . . Even to you. . . .

GIRL. Tell me, Sammy.

SAMMY. I didn't want people to know I was lonely. That I had no one . . . That I wasn't important.

GIRL. I'm not important either.

SAMMY. When they dropped that bomb . . . I was sixteen at the time . . . I came home. Home? It was a gap between a public baths and a surgical stores. Some man said: "What's the matter, sonny? Did you live here?" I looked at him. It was as if I heard my own voice talking. I meant to tell him the truth . . . But the words just came out. "Live here?" I said. "You think I'd live in a dump like this? No, I live the other side of the water. In S.W.3. And all my family's well." "You're lucky," he said. "Seems they've copped it down here."

GIRL. You said that? . . .

SAMMY. I didn't want him feeling sorry for me.

GIRL. But why?

SAMMY. After that, I got in the habit. I had nothing much to do in the evenings . . . Well, I'd look tired the morning after and say—"Was I on the town last night?" People respect you more if you act like that.

GIRL. Do they?

SAMMY. They don't say "Poor old Sammy Noles. *He* never gets an evening out." I hate anyone to say that. I hate to hear it.

GIRL. But to go as far as a wife . . .

SAMMY. Five years ago she cropped up. That Pheeming started her. I was late and he said, "What's the matter?

Wife overslept, did she?" "Yes," I said. "As a matter of
fact she did." It made me feel—as if I sort of belonged. It
was all right. Those first years I was married. Till the kids
started coming along.

GIRL. What happened then?

SAMMY. Getting them off to school in the mornings. Made
me constantly late for work.

GIRL. I see.

SAMMY. Of course, there was moments when I really enjoyed
my family life. Trips to the seaside . . . The first Christmas
after the youngest learnt to talk . . . Afternoons up the
river. . . .

GIRL (*suddenly losing patience*). Stop it! It was a fine excuse for
you. Better make up a wife than marry one.

SAMMY. I treated you badly, and yet, you know, since that
bomb . . . you're the first thing that happened to Sammy
Noles.

GIRL. Look at me, Sammy. We're really here. You and I. And
the bed's real. And the table. And the window. If I sit on
your feet you'll know I'm with you. I'll squash your feet.
That's a fact. You stupid man.

SAMMY. You couldn't trust me.

GIRL. What about me? Suppose I'm only after your passport.

SAMMY. I never thought that, honestly. Call me a liar. . . .

GIRL. Don't talk, Sammy. Don't talk so much. Let's live a
little while without talking about it. Keep quiet.

She puts her hand over his mouth.

We'll soon get it all straightened out.

Fade Out